PERGAMON INSTITUTE OF ENGLISH (OXFORD)

Language Teaching Methodology Series

Language and Literature Teaching

From Practice to Principle

Language and Literature Teaching

From Practice to Principle

CHRISTOPHER BRUMFIT

Professor of Education
University of Southampton

PERGAMON INSTITUTE OF ENGLISH

a member of the Pergamon Group

Oxford · New York · Toronto · Sydney · Frankfurt

U.K.	Pergamon Press Ltd., Headington Hill Hall, Oxford OX3 0BW, England
U.S.A.	Pergamon Press Inc., Maxwell House, Fairview Park, Elmsford, New York 10523, U.S.A.
CANADA	Pergamon Press Canada Ltd., Suite 104, 150 Consumers Road, Willowdale, Ontario M2J 1P9, Canada
AUSTRALIA	Pergamon Press (Aust.) Pty. Ltd., P.O. Box 544, Potts Point, N.S.W. 2011, Australia
FEDERAL REPUBLIC OF GERMANY	Pergamon Press GmbH, Hammerweg 6, D-6242 Kronberg-Taunus, Federal Republic of Germany

First edition 1985

Library of Congress Cataloguing in Publication Data

Brumfit, Christopher.
Language and literature teaching: from practice
to principle.
(Language teaching methodology series)
Bibliography: p.
Includes index.
1. Philology – Study and teaching.   I. Title.
II. Series.
P51.B779 1985   418'.007   85-3401

British Library Cataloguing in Publication Data

Brumfit, C. J.
Language and literature teaching : from
practice to principle. – (Language teaching
methodology series)
1. English language – Study and teaching –
Foreign speakers
I. Title   II. Series
428.2'4'07   PE1128.A2

ISBN 0-08-031551-8

*Printed and bound in Great Britain by
William Clowes Limited, Beccles and London*

To my colleagues in the Department of English for Speakers of Other Languages, University of London Institute of Education, 1974–1984. Their constant concern for the interface between theory and practice, and their willingness to argue the principles of our work at any time of day or night, have constantly renewed and improved my own efforts to be both principled and practical

Acknowledgements

As always, these papers owe many debts to many people. The principal debt, to my colleagues of the past decade, is acknowledged in the dedication. However, there are many other colleagues, from the British Council, TESOL, the British Association for Applied Linguistics, IATEFL and many conferences, workshops and meetings, who have contributed to this collection. Many students in London and overseas have disputed points and provided me with at least the illusion of clearer thinking, and editors of books and journals have helped with both content and style.

In addition, I am most grateful to Richard Rossner for permission to reprint a paper that we co-authored, to my son Simon for editorial help, to Vaughan James for encouragement in a variety of ways, and above all to my wife for her forbearance while I have tried to fit too much into too little time and energy.

The publisher is grateful to the following journals and publishers for permission to reproduce the previously published material included in this volume:

Applied Linguistics, BAAL Newsletter, ELT Documents, ELT Journal, Modern English Teacher, MEXTESOL Journal, Practical English Teacher, The School Librarian, SPEAQ Journal, On TESOL . . ., Triangle; Collins Publishers, Indiana University Press, Modern English Publications, Oxford University Press.

Contents

x   Contents

Introduction

This collection of papers, like its predecessor, *Problems and Principles in English Teaching*, Pergamon, 1980, constitutes an extended commentary on major issues in language and literature teaching, and teacher education for those fields, in the past decade. As it is a collection of papers, I have not tried to turn it into an extended book but have let the variety of occasions and audiences influence both style and content. Nonetheless, I hope that a consistent educational and applied linguistic position shows itself.

Some of the pieces here were delivered as keynote speeches at conferences, and some were deliberately tendentious pieces for non-academic journals. I have, however, retained the stylistic features of the originals in the hope that they give something of the flavour of the initial setting. Needless to say, the content is always entirely serious.

Certain themes are constantly visible, though I hope I have avoided too much exact repetition. There has been a concern to insist on the language as something potentially modifiable and usable by all who operate with it, whether learners or not; a concern with language as a vehicle for serious ideas and feelings; a concern with education as eventually a moral and ideological business. These concerns have led to criticism of analysts' categories in the construction of syllabuses, and of over-strong claims being made about what syllabuses can do for learners. They have also led to doubts about the trivialization of language teaching, even if it is done in the name of 'humanism' and resistance to the notion that market forces and education will never conflict. But above all else, these papers are concerned with trying to derive useful general principles, compatible with our fullest understanding of theory, from our current practice. Unless innovation builds on current practice, it is unlikely to succeed, and any reformer needs to understand the strengths, as well as the weaknesses, of the existing situation.

These papers are also appearing at what is, for me, the end of an era. As these go to press I am leaving the Institute of Education, London University, where I have been professionally very happy for the past ten years, to move to Southampton University. There I hope to increase my involvement with mother tongue teaching, and with language in education in general, without losing contact with overseas or the interests of language teachers. Both of the collections of papers from Pergamon contain items in these areas, of course, so I am not moving into an entirely new field.

Nonetheless, it is likely that much of my future work will be concentrating on multicultural education, the role of language in general education, and – I hope – on research in these fields and in language teaching methodology itself. This may well take me away from a specific concern of much of my previous work, the cluster of movements which can be gathered together under the heading of 'The Communicative Approach'. It will be clear from these and other papers that I have always been a slightly cautious and sceptical receiver of new ideas. On the other hand, I have been identified by some with the communicative approach because of the books I have written about it. Indeed, I was once accused within the same hour at a TESOL Convention of being an unthinking advocate of the communicative approach and of being its most virulent opponent! However, I only believe in movements as convenient historical fictions, ways of simplifying our view of the past. For the future, movements, packages and methods only have a role if we are trying to sell something by concealing the untidy truth and implying that language teaching can be made simple. But it cannot. I do believe that we can try to achieve good language teaching by looking for weaknesses in our current practices, and trying to remedy them. And I believe we should be imaginative and wide-ranging in our search for ideas to improve what we are doing; we should even look hard at the packages which people are anxious to sell us, for there may well be good in them, though not the whole truth that is claimed. But I do not believe we should try to be, or to train, or to write as, teachers of a particular method or movement. We should try to be good language teachers, and that will mean making different choices for each set of national conditions, for each type of school, for each set of students, and for each teaching personality. This is a heavy responsibility to place on teachers, but anything less would be to diminish them to cogs in a machine created by others and maintained by others. That cannot be good, either for teachers or learners. If we approach language teaching in a spirit of optimistic caution, we are unlikely to go wrong.

CJB

August 1984

COMMUNICATIVE LANGUAGE TEACHING

The first five papers are all concerned with the current state of language teaching, and particularly with the implications of our recognition that language is a fluid, dynamic and negotiable system. The early papers represent an attempt to integrate this view of language with the practical possibilities of conventional language teaching, and to consider some of the readjustments and difficulties that are emerging in practice. Several of the themes in these papers are taken up more academically in Section Three.

Teaching English to Speakers of Other Languages: the Position in the 1980s

(from *Practical English Teacher*, **1**, 1, October 1980)

Ten years ago, I suspect, it would have been much easier to provide an account of the state of EFL teaching. Today English is taught in so many places for so many different purposes and groups of people that it is very difficult to claim that there is widespread agreement about what we are doing. The teaching profession is divided and views about the relevance of linguistic theory to practical teaching differ greatly. After a period in which practising teachers were perhaps too ready to accept the advice of applied linguists who had rarely taught in the classroom, it is possible to see the opposite tendency appearing. Certainly, many of the more interesting developments in recent years have come out of teaching practice rather than theory.

There are dangers, of course, in ignoring theory altogether, but language teaching is less likely to follow the latest theoretical fashion than it was, and this development is unlikely to be harmful. Many of the more rigid 'rules' for good language teaching are being ignored as the complexity of language learning and behaviour is recognized more and more. Decisions about whether to allow mistakes to pass uncorrected or to use the mother tongue in the classroom are made on the basis of immediate need rather than dogma, and the teacher is both more confident in reacting to non-teaching experts and more humble in recognizing how little we really understand the process of learning and teaching language.

But this movement itself reflects changes in many disciplines outside language teaching. Linguists too recognize the complexity of language as it is used socially, and the difficulty of simplifying the learning process. Indeed, work during the past decade emphasizes more and more the social aspects of language use. In psychology, sociology and language teaching theory there have been developments which force us to consider the ways in which people use language rather than the formal structure of the language itself.

Communicative teaching

The movement that I have described above has shown itself in language teaching as what has been called 'the communicative movement' or 'the communicative approach'. This approach has tended to concentrate language teaching on the rules we need for using the language in social situations rather than the grammatical rules that we need to produce correct sentences. As a result, there have been a number of interesting practical developments, all of which are relevant to general language courses as well as specialized ones. Here is a list of the major developments:

3

1. The needs of the learners are analysed to find out what kinds of language use are most necessary for them.
2. The syllabus is specified not only in terms of the language items learners are likely to need, but also in terms of the kinds of meanings they may want to express ('notions') and the things they may want to do with their language ('functions').
3. Materials are developed which take into account the different ways in which people use language – they may be organized around topics, or functions of language – and they will be so organized that students are forced to try to express themselves through the language, often without much help from the teacher.
4. Teachers are trained to use group work and simultaneous pair work in class so that students have as many opportunities as possible to work intensively on their own.
5. Materials and techniques are devised to individualize work, so that all students in a class do not have to work in the same way, at the same pace, at the same time.
6. Language teaching is seen as an effort to involve 'the whole person', that is it cannot be treated as a purely technical exercise but should relate to students' genuine feelings, interests and needs.
7. It is assumed that students will necessarily make mistakes as they learn a new language, and that they need the opportunity to experiment with language, even if that means making mistakes while they do so.

Now of course throughout the seventies teachers continued to teach with procedures drawn from grammar-translation, direct and audiolingual methods – and no doubt from many others. Nonetheless, it is probably fair to say that all teachers will be influenced, if only indirectly, by the changes demanded by the communicative approach. Let us look at them in a little more detail.

Language as communication

Language performs two basic functions for human beings: it enables them to think in very complex ways by providing a structure for naming and expressing relationships between concepts, and it enables them to communicate with each other. These two basic functions are obviously closely related to each other, and a child learning a mother tongue learns how to communicate at the same time as learning culturally appropriate ways of thinking. The second language learner, however, starts learning with an already developed ability to think and speak. Furthermore, while young children inevitably grow up as members of the society whose language they are learning, second language learners only rarely wish to become assimilated into the culture of the target language. Most often, the purpose of learning a foreign language is to make contact with the inhabitants, the culture, the literature or the science of another country.

This has two important implications for language teaching. First, it suggests that learners will need to understand and interact with the foreign culture, and second that they will need to be able to express themselves *as themselves*, as non-members of the foreign country – that is, in some sense, they must learn to express ideas and feelings which are not normally expressed in the target language. A German learning English, for example, will want to be able to express in English ideas which are German ideas, for which there is no conventional English means of expression. That is to say that we want to teach people to *use* foreign languages for their own purposes, and not merely to *possess* them for the purposes already developed by native speakers. We want learners, as themselves, to be able to communicate as fully as they feel the need to, in the foreign language.

The implication of this argument is that we are more concerned with what people do with language than with what they know of it, and recent developments in the philosophy of language and in sociolinguistics have helped us to understand 'how to do things with words'. To give a few very simple examples, *Can you put the shopping in the car?* usually means in English not 'Are you able to put the shopping in the car?' but 'Will you . . .?'. It is a request for help, not information and cannot be interpreted without an understanding of the conventions linking language form with language function. *Would you like to do the next sentence?* when said by a teacher to a pupil will normally be an order, not a request. *Watch out!* will normally be a warning, in spite of its imperative form, and will only be an order in specific circumstances. In each of these cases, understanding is dependent on our knowledge of rules of use as well as rules of grammar.

Now, if the words and grammatical patterns of a language had clear-cut, one-to-one meanings, it would not be difficult to learn a new language, but nor would it be possible to say anything original; new messages would be almost impossible to construct. What we in fact do (in any language) is *negotiate* our meaning by interacting and adjusting to the shared knowledge, the assumptions, even the linguistic ability, of the person we are talking to. Even in reading or writing we are constantly trying to interpret the intentions or interpretations of the writer or reader and adjusting ourselves accordingly. Of course, we need our understanding of the vocabulary and structure of the language before we can negotiate meaning well, but we have to learn the process of negotiation if we are to be able to communicate effectively.

Communicative teaching aims to assist this process in the classroom.

What kind of syllabus?

Until the last decade or so, it was generally assumed that language learners had to learn the vocabulary and grammar of the language, and then, by practising, learn how to use them. Syllabuses would normally consist of inventories of vocabulary and grammar items. The grammatical items ('structures' or 'sentence patterns') would be ordered to form a structural syllabus. Indeed, most syllabuses are still of this kind, and arguments are still going on about what, if any, are the drawbacks of such organization.

It is possible to conceive of at least two other ways of organizing language for classroom use. One possibility is to concentrate on ordering the situations or settings in which language might be used. However, it is difficult to see how such situations can really develop progressively through a long course, or how generalizable the language learnt will be. The other possibility would be to produce what has been called a *notional/functional syllabus*. Such a syllabus, it has been suggested, would consist of an ordering, not of structural items, but of *functions* of language (advising, requesting, persuading, etc.) and semantic *notions* (concepts like time, place, etc.) as they are expressed in the language. There is a strong current debate over how likely it is that we shall ever produce a syllabus which truly develops along functional/notional lines rather than grammatical ones. But what is certain is that many teachers and materials writers have found it helpful to think more systematically than was previously possible, and this is a result of various tentative suggested lists of notions and functions. Certainly at an advanced level, when the basic grammatical system has been learnt, a functional and/or notional organization will be extremely valuable.

The main argument for a functional/notional approach is that learners need language to express meanings and to do things in the real world, they do not want language in order to display grammatical patterns. For this reason, it is suggested, such a syllabus would correspond more closely to the needs of the learner and consequently motivation to learn would improve. Opponents have argued that grammar is the economical system which underlies all language use, and that lists of notions and functions cannot be expressed through a convenient system, so that we do not know how different functions relate to each other enough to be able to construct a coherent syllabus. On this issue the debate continues, but there is no doubt that syllabuses for all learners are now more likely to be specified in terms of functions, settings, types of interaction and subject matter, as well as grammatical and lexical levels. This does not necessarily mean, of course, that such behavioural features were ignored in all earlier syllabuses: often it was assumed that the syllabus should specify the language items only, and the teaching procedures used (contextualizing, meaningful practice) should make the language effective in use.

What kind of materials?

Recent developments in technology have made possible a much wider range of facilities for classroom teachers than were available even a few years ago. It is now usual to find courses accompanied by cassette recordings, and video materials are being used increasingly. Yet teachers probably still have to rely on the most efficient and most accessible device of all, the textbook.

Textbooks, too, have been updated by technology, however. Attractive design with plentiful colour and illustrations and diagrams is now commonplace. In tune with contemporary ideas of communication, many textbooks are now much more dependent on tasks (involving such activities as filling in charts, interviewing, interpreting various forms of popular journalism, etc.) than on the rather stolid reading matter of the past. There is an enormous wealth of original and creative ideas available in textbooks, and they now limit themselves far less to the formal linguistic system. They may, for example, include exercises for relaxation, material for mime or suggestions for mother tongue reading. There have been gains and losses in this change, and it may be worth making a few comments.

First, the gains in attractiveness are considerable, and along with that has gone a greater responsibility by writers for the whole process of learning, both formally and informally. However, the concentration on interaction has resulted in neglect of other equally important concerns. Subject matter has very often been relatively trivial, and at a *Reader's Digest* level. Serious topics are frequently touched upon, especially important contemporary socio-political issues, but they are rarely treated profoundly. The understandable wish to produce something genuinely interesting often results in material which is superficial rather than demanding. Yet one of the implications of the 'whole person' approach is that foreign language learning should enable us to acquire genuinely new information as we learn, so that we engage through the foreign language with material of compelling interest. Compelling interest is not the same thing as superficial excitement. There has also been a tendency to see British culture largely in terms of a (rather out-of-date) 'swinging London' image, and student interest, at school level, in terms of football and pop music. All of these have a place, but not to the exclusion of most other topics.

But it is certainly true to say that now teachers have a much wider choice of material than in the past, that it is more imaginative, more flexible, more attractively produced than it was – and more expensive! Such materials are also more demanding on the teacher, for their very flexibility forces teachers to make choices of principle about their classroom procedures all the time. It is to this issue that we now turn.

What kind of methods?

An emphasis on communication has several immediate implications for methodology, though none of them is very radical – there is no fundamentally new communicative methodology. However, simultaneous pair and group activity in class, with all groups or pairs working and talking at once, becomes central as a procedure, for only thus can quasi-realistic communication be conveniently simulated on a large scale, and only thus can intense personal contact between the learners and the language they create be fostered. Role play and simulation exercises become important, and the classroom is bound to become less teacher-centred, as small group interactions, and materials-centred work become more widespread. Teachers now find themselves using any procedure which will help to make language work meaningful. These may include activities often frowned upon in the past: for example, time may be given for students to think silently about appropriate and truthful answers to questions, which may be produced in uncertain language; the mother tongue may be used, even for translation, when it contributes to more fluent communication; and students may be encouraged to talk freely for much of the time without too much concern for precise accuracy.

The purpose of all these procedures is the same: to contribute towards the creation of a genuine language-using community (if only a very simple one) in the classroom. In such a community students are involved as far as possible in language use which means something to them, expressing their own thoughts or feelings. They are encouraged to experiment and play with the language they hear or read so that they can begin to develop it for their own needs, right from the beginning of their learning, and they are encouraged to help each other in doing this. The positive attitude and approach of the teacher will be essential support as students develop confidence and competence. But the teacher will still be able to offer generalizations and rules in answer to students' requests and will be a resource as well as an organizer of activities.

There is thus no great revolution in methodology, but a concentration on many techniques which some teachers have been using for years. It is true that there are a number of specific 'methods' available (The Silent Way, Counselling Learning, Suggestopedia) which offer very clear, and often rather idiosyncratic organization for teaching in order to achieve similar ends. But such approaches sometimes lead to dogmatism among their followers, and can rarely be imposed directly on conventional school classrooms on a large scale. The underlying principles of such 'humanistic' approaches are simply the principles which will underly any good communicative teaching.

What kind of teacher?

It is probably a fair generalization that teachers of English as a Foreign Language have become more and more highly trained during the past decade. Certainly, as this article has tried to show, there has been a wealth of discussion and new ideas. And the more discussion there is, the more confusing it can be to new teachers. What are we demanding of our teachers? Perhaps it is worth making a few suggestions.

1. Teachers should like their students, and if they do not, they should disguise it so well that no-one else realizes.
2. They should be as clear as possible about why their students are learning English.
3. They should be clear to themselves about their beliefs on the nature of language learning and teaching.
4. They should be always open and free in discussion and help their colleagues, senior and junior.
5. They should be professionally well-informed.
6. Their approach to teaching should be founded on principles without being dogmatic, flexible without being merely fashionable.
7. They should be constantly trying to improve.
8. They should be humble, willing to recognize the merits of the past as well as the present, and the wisdom of the outside critic as well as the professional.

In short, teachers should be terrifyingly perfect, but it will not hurt us to admit that fact. These eight points would all have applied just as much ten years ago. Ideas on teaching may change, but the demands, and nature of the job remain the same. Fortunately, the professional prospects look bright.

Accuracy and Fluency: a fundamental distinction for communicative teaching methodology

(adapted from *Practical English Teacher*, **1**, 3, February 1981)

The last ten years have seen a great deal of discussion of 'Communicative Language Teaching', but almost all the discussion has concentrated on how to organize syllabuses and materials. There has been much less consideration of direct classroom activity by the teacher. Usually, when methodological procedures are referred to at all, a brisk reference is made to the need for more group work, or the use of role-play, and the reader is left in suspense.

One reason for this neglect of methodology is that communication has always been one of the main concerns of practising teachers, and a 'communicative' methodology is unlikely to be completely new – it is more likely to involve an increase in importance for some techniques at the expense of others than a total reorganization of classroom activities. But at the same time a truly communicative methodology may also involve teachers looking at their task in ways which may differ substantially from those of the past.

Generally, standard foreign language teaching has always acted as if students learn small units very carefully and gradually build them up until they have acquired a fairly full language system which they can then use in more or less realistic situations. The assumption has been that teachers should expose students to the language (especially through reading) in a fairly uncontrolled way, but that students' learning and use of the language should be restricted to what the teachers allow. Learning, that is, is based on accurate reproduction of items of language presented by the teacher, or the textbook.

Such accuracy, of course, can reflect a number of different systems. A sentence like

> *This is a ridiculous discussion*

can be judged as inaccurate, when produced by a student, from the points of view of pronunciation, grammar, choice of words, or appropriacy to context. Such a judgement, however, will always be based on the formal properties of the language system – the sound system for pronunciation, the grammatical, lexical and communication systems for the others. Let us consider briefly some of the implications of judgements of this kind.

Natural communication and linguistic rules

Supposing you were having a natural conversation with someone in your mother tongue, and supposing – as you were talking – the other person stopped you by saying, 'Just a moment! That sentence wasn't quite correct', or 'You didn't pronounce that word quite right, did you?' If this happened you would be entitled to feel very annoyed, and for a very good reason. Conversation is not normally intended to show off ability in grammar or pronunciation, and if the person you are speaking to stops listening to *what* you say and starts commenting on *how* you say it, you will feel that they are not interested in you and your ideas, but only in scoring points off you, that they are not treating you seriously.

Teachers, of course, are paid to help learners to produce correct forms in foreign languages, and a teacher who absolutely refused to correct would send students off to reference books in their own time, for learners must be given help in forming correct utterances. But they are also paid to help learners to communicate naturally, and this aspect of their work has received less attention. The problem is that no-one can communicate naturally and at the same time concentrate fully on the form rather than the content of their speech. It is not just that we do not comment on the formal features of someone's speech without appearing rude, but we do not even think about them. When we are taking part in the conversation, our concern is with how much we need to say to make our point clear, with how much knowledge we share with the other person, and we adjust what we say to fit in with this. We do not want to waste time and effort by providing too much information, and nor do we want to provide so little that we shall be unclear. At the same time, we do not want to appear rude, and thus cause the conversation to fail, and nor do we want to draw special attention to the way we speak, and thus distract attention from our message. (Of course, there *are* occasions when we may intend to confuse our listeners, or to be rude, but when we do this we are deliberately breaking the rules of normal conversation in order to make a particular point.) When we hold a conversation, we normally co-operate with the people we are talking to, in order to reach an agreed goal – this may be the obtaining of a piece of information, the enjoying of a joke, sharing a memory, explaining a process or any other purpose. In order to do this effectively speakers perform an unconscious guessing game, for they have to establish what the agreed goal is (and this is not always clear, especially at the beginning of a conversation), as well as how much knowledge, or past experience, or understanding, is shared by the other partners in the conversation.

Now, of course, while we are doing all this we are obeying linguistic rules: that is, we are observing the shared conventions of the nature of the language we are speaking. But, just as we have to negotiate about shared information, so we have to negotiate about shared conventions. We know, in general, that we share the basic principles of grammar, that most of the words we use mean more or less the same, and that we shall use more or less the same strategies for explaining and illustrating our ideas. But we cannot assume that we share such features in every detail. Words from specialized dialects – perhaps regional or social, perhaps semi-private slang expressions, perhaps technical vocabulary – may occur in the other person's speech, or words which both people share may be used with slightly different meanings. Indeed, a lot of academic work is precisely about the different ways in which words are used, and the different ideas communicated by the same words. Philosophers have discussed at great length the meaning of such terms as 'honesty' or 'beauty', and many books have been written about how the meanings of words have changed through the ages. Although change is slow, it is present all the time, and we have to learn to recognize subtle differences in the ways we use words.

Much the same principles apply to grammatical rules, and indeed to all features of language. As language users, we adapt ourselves to constantly changing patterns, and the words we use have meaning in relation to the contexts we use them in. I have several times asked during a lecture, 'Has anyone got a pencil?' and always more people offer me pens than pencils. Quite correctly, they are interpreting 'pencil' as 'something to write with' in the context.

And on top of all this there is the problem of interpreting the cultural, rather than the literal significance of terms being used. In many contexts, in Britain at least, 'I must have a drink' implies an alcoholic drink, while the size and time of the meal, 'tea', varies greatly from one part of Britain to another. Both within and across languages there are vast differences to be understood, even at this straightforward level, before we start thinking about the more complicated matters of metaphorical usage, or of the conventional significance of particular utterances. (Is 'Why don't you come round to my place sometime?' a serious invitation or a piece of conventional politeness?)

An understanding of linguistic rules on their own, or even of the rules of social interaction, will not enable us to use a language effectively: we need to be able to adapt and improvise – that is, to conduct our own negotiations.

The language teacher's role

Part of the language teacher's responsibility must remain that of presenting the linguistic system to the students in a way that makes it as easy as possible for them to learn it. But the traditional classroom procedures of presentation, drilling and practice will not in themselves enable students to learn even the linguistic system, let alone how to use it easily. These traditional procedures may assist students to store parts of the language in their memories, but until the language has been activated so that it can be used (either for easy recognition or production) it cannot be considered fully learnt. Experienced teachers will know that the time-lag between 'teaching' and genuine 'use' will vary enormously from student to student, and from language item to language item. A few items, clearly-understood technical terms for example, may be used very soon after initial teaching, but for most items we may have to wait six weeks or more before students will start producing them naturally, without prior thought. The teacher therefore has a responsibility to create plenty of opportunities for students to use – or negotiate with – the language they have learnt or been exposed to. Such opportunities can be provided by fluency work, in which students are expected to concentrate on the communication task, on the use of language, and not on formal accuracy.

The syllabus and fluency activities

Syllabuses usually specify what the teacher has to teach. A great deal of work in class, however, must be concerned not with teaching, but learning. One of the teacher's biggest difficulties is that a learner's speed of learning is different from the teacher's speed of teaching. What is needed could be described as 'a syllabus with gaps', or 'a syllabus with holes in it'. There will clearly have to be an important place in the syllabus for the introduction of new language, but there must also be extensive 'gaps' in which no new material is presented, but students are enabled to use effectively what they have learnt, from whatever source they have learnt it, to develop the skills of negotiation by talking with each other for more or less genuine purposes. During this period of fluency activity the teacher will not be able to predict the nature of the language being used. The learners will have the opportunity to use any language which comes to them naturally, however full of mistakes it may seem to be from the point of view of formal accuracy. They will thus have experience of genuine language behaviour – adjusting, negotiating meaning, trying to say things they have not been taught to say – with the limited dialect of English that they have so far developed. They will be learning how to be fluent, not through formal teaching, but through practice exercising the innate ability which they have already developed in their mother tongue, but adjusting this in part to the demands of English. In this way, students will be able – at the very least – to make maximally effective use of the language they have learnt, while it is possible that they may improve their development of the formal system itself by increased experience of communication.

Right from the beginning of the course, about a third of the total time could be spent on this sort of fluency activity, and the proportion will inevitably increase as time goes on.

Types of fluency task

Teachers have used many forms of fluency activity for a long time. Nearly all tasks which involve simultaneous pairs practice, or simultaneous group work, will have an element of fluency discussion included. So, too, will many simulation and role-play activities, and many communication games. But such procedures will only incorporate fluency activity if students – whatever the task – are attempting to co-operate, using English as much as possible, with no fear of correction if they make mistakes. If this is accepted, though, there is no need for fluency work to incorporate games or meaningless competitive tasks. Any language exercises can be discussed in small groups, and very traditional textbooks have been used successfully as a basis for communicative work of this kind. It is largely a matter of the teacher being aware of the need to devote a major proportion of class time to fluency work as well as accuracy.

Getting fluency accepted

Many teachers feel that they are forced by students to correct their English all the time. When this is likely, it is worth spending some time explaining to students exactly why it is necessary to have some experience of working fluently with English as well as accurately. The kind of arguments outlined at the beginning of this article are worth offering to students. It needs to be emphasized that everyone, in any language, needs to develop the skills of adjustment and negotiation. Such development must, however, be accompanied by organized exposure to good models of English, both in speech and writing; otherwise a fluent classroom dialect may develop which bears little resemblance to English as spoken by competent native or non-native speakers. There is no question of fluency being in any way a substitute for accuracy. Both are essential.

Some teachers and students are worried by the possibility of errors being constantly reinforced by repetition in fluency work. It is probably true to say that the dangers of repetition of errors leading to bad habits was greatly exaggerated in the past, but the risk is best avoided by allowing really serious and widespread errors to be drilled out during the accuracy part of the course. On the whole, the process of trying to create the language they need to communicate is more likely to help learners to develop a native-speaker-like system than pure habit-formation procedures. But fluency work will not provide a wonder cure for language learning ills – nothing will – and it is discussed here simply with the aim of improving our approaches to methodological problems.

At the same time, though, I would want to suggest that more successful communicative teaching will occur if teachers think carefully of developing methodologies for both accuracy and fluency, than if all the syllabuses in the world were restructured notionally.

See Brumfit, 1984, for an academic development of this position.

Ideology, Communication and Learning to Use English

(from *English Language Teaching Journal*, *34, 3, 1980*)

At the Oxford conference of IATEFL in January 1977 I delivered a paper with a similar title to that of this one (Brumfit, 1978). I wish now to pick up some of the problems posed at the end of that paper and develop them more fully. Particularly, I want to consider some of the justifications for the use of exploratory procedures in language teaching, and some of the limitations on their use. First, though, it may be useful to summarize the argument.

What is being identified as the 'communicative' movement in language teaching is a response to a number of different influences. Partly it results from our increased ability to describe and specify exactly what takes place in a communicative act, both linguistically and socially. Partly it is a response to demands from learners for courses which reflect the anticipated communication needs of specific groups of learners. And partly it reflects a dissatisfaction with a 'package' view of language learning, that is one which appears to pass over to the learner a package of knowledge of language (or language use) which at the beginning is possessed by the teacher and at the end is possessed by the student. There are of course other factors in the development of the communicative movement, but it is this third one I want to concentrate on here.

It has for years been argued that language teachers are concerned with teaching the *use* of language, not the ability to repeat rules of grammar. Even the strongest audio-lingual arguments were primarily about how best to do this rather than whether to do it, and in many ways recent discussion largely reflects the same preoccupations. It is often implied that the syllabus-designer needs to specify a system which describes the target language, to find ways of helping learners to learn this system, and then to leave them to it. There is widespread agreement that the system should now be functional and/or notional and/or grammatical, but it is still frequently assumed that in some way the system can be taught on the basis of descriptions made by linguists, or social psychologists, or some other kind of scientist.

Now, no-one will be justified in abolishing some form of input at early stages in language learning. The vital question is the status of this input. Is it by definition something alien, gibberish which can only later become meaningful, or can learners begin to use it very rapidly? Traditional attitudes to language and culture have generally made us assume that foreign languages are necessarily alien and must be approached from the outside. The learner is always placed in a deficit position. But in what sense is English the possession of those who already speak it? If language is viewed as an object which you can either have or not have, the learner is in a genuine position of deficit. But if we accept that all human beings possess a language faculty, and that the characteristics of a particular language are

14

determined by the universal constraints imposed by the structure of the human brain combined with the local constraints imposed by the culture within which it is used, then we must also accept

(i) that all human beings are equipped *before they start learning* with a great deal of implicit understanding of any new language; and

(ii) that the learning of the new language must be intimately bound up with the process of operating in a new culture.

It follows from (i) above that there will be some things about operating in the new language which we shall not need to teach—in other words we do not need to accept for teaching all the information linguists provide us with about what it means to use a language effectively. But let us consider what is meant in (ii) by 'operating in a new culture'.

Every time we try to communicate with someone else, we are involved in a limited cross-cultural operation: we are operating a co-operative principle to achieve enough overlap with the intentions and needs of another person for a mutually convenient solution to be reached. Now most of the time, of course, all participants in a conversation know what is being talked about adequately for the needs of the situation. We need very little 'negotiation' to interpret 'Pass me a pencil, please', though even here we may need *some* 'negotiation', for we may interpret a 'pencil' as 'something to write with' and pass a pen, which may provoke the reply 'Not that, a pencil', continuing the 'negotiation'. This is a personal and temporary example: 'pencil' may not need to be distinguished from 'pen' for the purposes of this interaction. But this illustrates our tolerance with meaning. We do not treat messages as if they have fixed, permanent, and rigid meanings. And as soon as we move on to more sophisticated examples, for example in philosophical or political discussion, or in legal disputes, or even in family arguments, it becomes clear that the same combinations of words may be extremely difficult to define, even within a specific context.

The situation is complicated by the fact that, as we move further and further away from home, the assumptions we can take for granted with fellow speakers are reduced in number. This is partly because language operates within a general system of symbols derived from the world around us, and uses items such as associations of particular heraldic symbols, references to people and places (whether historical or fictional), slang, in-jokes, and so on. All of these may have a significance which is hidden to the outsiders, even if they speak the 'same' language. But, even worse, such apparently temporary associations may become embedded in the language long after their specific reference has disappeared, and such embedding may become part of the standard language, understood by most speakers, or may remain local and dialectal. Further, the relationship between the individual 'pencil/pen'-type negotiation, the immediate symbolic reference and the embedded and frozen reference is in a constant state of flux. This is because the people who use the language are human beings, with individual and corporate motivations, preoccupations and needs, and they *use* the language to express those constantly changing motivations, preoccupations, and needs, both individually and as groups. Nor does it matter whether the people using the language have it as a mother tongue or as a second or even a foreign language. No one will stop those who wish to use it from using it, and insofar as they communicate with others, they will contribute to the changing language.

It is important to emphasize that people *use* language, rather than *have* language, and it is important to emphasize that as they use it they create new things from it, as the craftsman does with clay. Just as we respond to works of art, and not to the substance from which they are made, so we respond to—and adapt, destroy, and play with—the language we have inherited, without insisting that it be viewed as some original, unmoulded, uncreated substance.

It is also important to see that, whether we like it or not, the foreign learner of English is by the act of starting to learn the language entering one part of English culture, not as an outsider but as a participant. The extent of the participation will be controlled primarily by the learner's ability to communicate with other English users—but when communication can take place, a community, and a sub-culture, is being formed and the language will be used to express messages appropriate to the users, exploiting their own cultural needs and assumptions through the medium of English. The crucial point is, of course, 'when communication can take place', for insofar as the learners can communicate beyond the immediate environment, they will be extending their cultural range to wider and wider contexts—and, with English teaching, such contexts will tend to approximate to the major centres of English use, the major English-speaking nations. Thus the learners can be said to be extending their natural ability to negotiate through language to new cultural contexts, as they acquire English. (But note that the culture is not the same as the language: Chinese physicists may enter the culture of American physicists, within the domain of science, more easily than they may, within that same domain, enter the culture of fellow Chinese-speaking non-scientists.) To find out how much knowledge is shared, to recognize how much flexibility and tolerance in meaning is appropriate for a particular situation, and to acquire strategies for matching one's own understanding with that demanded by the situation, is a task for native and non-native speakers alike. Part of foreign-language teaching must cater for this.

The whole of the preceding argument has been designed to show that there is an intimate relationship between what we need to express—our feelings, philosophy, ideology, political and religious beliefs, as well as more mundane matters—and the language we use. Now since all of these are major areas in which different cultures separated themselves from each other, it follows that as teachers we should not be teaching students to adopt the philosophies, ideologies, and so on of native speakers, but enabling them to express their own through English, and to understand other people's. That is, we should teach them to *use* the language for *their own purposes.* All of which has major implications for our teaching methodology, for we need strategies which will enable learners to become fluent in whatever language they have got, using that language to express things from themselves, not from the teacher.

It is for these reasons that there is now an increasing emphasis not only on role play and simulation activities but also on exploratory language work, in which students are encouraged to talk about projects without careful control by the teacher. Mistakes will constantly occur, but—for *this* part of the work at least—they will not matter: the important thing is that students learn to experience using their own language without feeling inhibited by the possibility of correction. Only thus will they feel confident enough to learn to develop further with their own English language, not the English that belongs to the teacher.

Of course there is still a major need for language to be presented to students, and for an emphasis on accuracy in much of the work, but for true internalization a great deal of fluency work will be necessary, and students must be told that sometimes they need to learn to grope and explore with language, and to be given plenty of opportunities to do so. Formal, often traditional, exercises will have their place for some of the presentation work in many schools, and for much remedial work—learning will not be *entirely* through fluency—but the student who has never learnt to talk naturally, in obviously foreign but still understandable English, has only learnt to imitate the language, not to use it.

Communicative Language Teaching: problems and prospects 预景

(plenary address to the MEXTESOL Annual National Convention, Acapulco, September 1980. A slightly different version was published in the *Mextesol Journal*, **5**, 2, 1981)

It is an honour and a pleasure to address MEXTESOL, and to renew so many old acquaintances. It is also a rather awesome responsibility to speak first at a convention such as this, for presenting a plenary poses several major difficulties. Here is the outsider (very frequently), called in with more or less understanding of the local scene, expected to produce a talk which is general enough to appeal to all who listen, and also specific enough to provide some intellectual satisfaction. Altogether, this is a daunting task, in which the speaker is forced to tread a delicate path between the various dangers of cliché, vapid generalization, and irrelevance.

Plenary speeches tend to fall into a number of set patterns, with which we are all too familiar. There is the inspirational-pessimistic ('we have nothing to offer but blood, toil, sweat and tears, but we shall overcome . . .') and the inspirational-optimistic ('we must all work together towards the glorious future which is ours . . .'), both of which make us feel big, hopeful—especially the pessimistic one—and truly human; teachers need to be reminded of their humanity. Then there is the devotional-mystical ('students *are* real people, *whole* people . . .') which has an avant-garde variant ('*teachers* are whole people . . .'). These make us feel sensitive, complete and more truly human. But other plenaries are intended to make us feel small and incomplete. Their way of being general is to be so precise that they are equally irrelevant to all their hearers. Here we find the devotional-psychometric ('we thus *know* that a group of 11 male Egyptian Arabic speakers will experience on the average in 74% of cases some difficulty with . . .'), and the public-relational-hyperbolic ('this is the greatest project in international relations ever conceived, never have so many been brought into the classroom for the benefit of so few . . .'), and no doubt many more.

In this paper I want to be both big *and* small. I want to look at our current model of language, and to see it in the context of our general understanding of human beings, as we view them in 1980. Such a discussion may make us feel small, because we shall realize how little we really know. But it should also make us feel optimistic, as we realize how much we succeed in doing in spite of not understanding fully what it is we do. There are grounds for pessimism of the intellect, but also for optimism of the will.

Attitudes to language in the 1970s

The last ten years have seen a major shift in approaches to language which, for language teaching, may constitute a more genuine paradigm shift than anything that came in with transformational grammar. Let me start to consider it right outside language altogether. In a recent, much praised book Robert A. Hinde asked:

> Can we build a science, in the sense of an integrated body of knowledge, concerned with relationships between individuals? (Hinde, 1979: 5)

Yet clearly if we are to gain any really helpful understanding of language as our students expect to use it, our understanding must be within the context of human relationships. Certainly, throughout the 1970s, linguists have found themselves increasingly concerned with the context of linguistic patterning. Syntactic studies lead inevitably into semantic studies, and semantic studies take us towards social context. It is by no means clear that linguistics can be, in any sense, an autonomous science; nor is it clear that its links are stronger with psychology than with sociology. Language studies have been caught up in the disputes between sociologists over the most appropriate conceptual frameworks to use and the drift towards the social sciences is resulting in a reappraisal of what it is for linguistics to be 'scientific', for the human sciences have conspicuously failed when they have attempted to take over models from the exact sciences.

This process is reflected in language teaching in increasing uncertainty over idealized models for teaching purposes. We are beginning to see such models as devices to assist the study of linguistics, but not necessarily as devices which are directly useful to learners of languages. We have less security, as a result of our more sophisticated understanding of variation in language. And to the extent that that makes us less dogmatic, it is good. It is bad, however, insofar as it leads us to abdicate our responsibility to provide a coherent and principled approach to language teaching.

The direct impact of the paradigm shift I have referred to has been to transfer our interest from language as a product, idealized into a discrete system, to language as a process of human interaction, a product of social and personal needs. This has led to two kinds of solution to teaching problems being proposed. One is to attempt to concentrate still on the idealized model of language, but to idealize in terms of the meanings being conveyed ('notions') or in terms of what is done with the language in interaction ('functions'). The other is to concentrate more fully on the strategies adopted by learners, as they make their language meaningful (one of the various competing definitions of 'discourse'). The latter approach, particularly, has considerable implications for teaching methodology. Both of these would claim that they are concerned with language as something we 'do' rather than something we 'have', but the former concerns itself with a description of the 'doing' and the latter with the process itself.

Attitudes to language teaching

This shift can be seen underlying a whole range of preoccupations of language teachers during the past decade. Our work is allegedly more learner-centred now. The basis of teaching languages for specific purposes (ESP) is a concern for what particular groups of students need to do with their language in order to perform social roles. Functional-notional syllabuses base their justification on their greater sensitivity to linguisitic performance rather than linguistic knowledge. The idea of a Threshold Level assumes the need for a specified level of competence to enable students to perform certain activities in the language. Acquisition studies, and the concurrent development of theoretical constructs such as interlanguage, assume a concern for language in a condition of change, by definition unstable. And methodological discussion assumes, more frequently than in the past, that teachers should not control the linguistic output from students. Group work, free discussion, role-play and simulation activities are expected in even the most traditional classes, and whole methodologies have been devoted to the problem of increasing total commitment of learners so that the language comes from them and not from the teacher or textbook.

It would be unwise to over-emphasize the similarities between these various positions. However, they do share a number of features. They remove the focus from the teacher to the learner, and from the structure of the language to the process of linguistic interaction. Recently, however, a number of writers have expressed concern about a concentration on peripheral aspects of language learning at the expense of essential ones. It may not be sufficient to master the grammatical and phonological systems, but it is certainly necessary. The problem is that—given the enormous range and variability of linguistic performance—it is difficult to concentrate on these aspects without producing a model which is rigid and idealized and ignores precisely the variable features to which we have recently become sensitive. Do we have to choose between the communicative insights of the present and the grammatical insights of the past? It is not uncommon to assume that we do, but such an assumption is surely simplistic.

A methodological solution

One possible solution is to concentrate on methodology. This has several merits. It concentrates on something which is within the control of the teacher. It enables us to integrate insights deriving from experience of teaching with those that have a theoretical basis, and it is by definition functional, concerned with human activity, for methodology rests solely in the relationships between the inhabitants of classrooms. There is one other advantage which is worth mentioning, also, and that is that a concentration on methodology forces us to keep our theoretical constructs simple. Our categories are consumer-based and the consumer is the teacher, that is someone who has a job to do and is concerned with effective organization rather than conceptual certainty. We need categories which make sense in practice, and which relate to the theory, but above all they must enable teacher education and teacher discussion and thinking to be efficient. Consequently, the constructs must combine practical applicability with clarity and conceptual simplicity.

One convenient way of doing this is to concentrate on the two goals of language teaching, *accuracy* and *fluency*. Wilga Rivers referred to essentially the same distinction, though in rather more behaviourist terms, when she talked about 'skill-getting' and 'skill-using' (Rivers, 1972: 22). The traditional language classroom has assumed a static, idealized model of the language, and has taught this to students, concentrating on the accuracy of what they produce (in terms of grammar, pronunciation, lexical choice and appropriate stylistic choice). Although procedures which develop fluency have always occurred, particularly in reading and writing, they have often been subordinated to the need to develop accurate mastery of the code. Only occasionally, for example in relation to extensive reading and creative writing, has fluency been given a specific place in teaching. It would not be unfair to summarize the assumptions of teachers and methodologists by saying that learners should first become accurate, usually bit by bit, in the code, and then learn to speed up, and to use skills in combination, so that they gradually become fluent. Fluency is thus conceived of as essentially a matter of speeding up what has already been mastered accurately.

But what if fluent language use is qualitatively different from self-consciously accurate use? If we see language use as essentially interactive, and the form as a product of that interactive process between speaker and speaker, or between writer and reader, then mastery of the formal possibilities in the abstract takes us only part of the way towards being fluent. We cannot operate with tokens that we are unaware of (so the teacher has an obligation to present the formal features of the language in as learnable a way as possible), but we must also have the opportunity to use those tokens in life-like interaction. And it is possible that the process of learning the tokens effectively will depend on our being able to experience using them fluently as well as having some awareness of accurate forms. Altogether, whether we take a strong fluency position, arguing that fluency work is necessary for most students to enable them to use the language accurately, or a weak position, arguing that even if they can acquire an accurate appreciation of the code by other means, such accuracy must be transformed to fluency by the use of appropriate methodological procedures, in either case we must allow fluency work an important position. Fluency work will occur only when students are using the language in the same way as they use their mother tongues—that is to say when they are using it as part of interaction, or as a means of conceptual clarification, without being concerned primarily with whether it fulfils externally-imposed formal requirements. Thus fluency work will be a side-product of small-group work, when discussion takes place in the target language, and will occur during improvization in role-play exercises, whenever silent extensive reading is being performed, or writing for a purpose of realistic communication. It will be characterized by adaptation to the rapidly changing relationship between speakers, or between writer and reader, by negotiation of meaning, by reorganization of assumptions, by errors in terms of formal accuracy which will only be corrected if they impair communicative efficiency, and by a concern with the message rather than the medium. The criteria for error will thus be difficult to ascertain, for they will vary according to the differences between participants, topic, setting and all the other constraints on the speech event. Any attempt to intervene and correct during fluency activities will therefore raise difficulties, for in normal life to concentrate on the medium at the expense of the message is usually rather rude. It is worth trying the experiment of correcting the pronunciation, or the grammar of a close relation for a few moments in order to appreciate the tension that can rapidly build up by consistently breaking the discourse rule that we attend primarily to the message as co-operatively as we can.

Now it is of course true that teachers are paid partly to perform this kind of rudeness on students. Students rightly demand feedback, and there must be times when it is provided. And a great deal of this feedback must be concerned with the accuracy of a student's mastery of the code. But the code cannot be an end in itself, only a means to an end. Students need to know, and—even more—teachers need to know exactly when accuracy is being pursued and when fluency is. Accuracy work may be very traditional and formal, and will be corrected, by the teacher or by students themselves. It is an essential part of language learning. But it is not enough in itself, and a substantial part of class time needs to be devoted to fluency work in which students behave as nearly as they can in native-speaker-like ways in whatever dialect of English they have so far developed. Whether we class what they produce as dialect or interlanguage is unimportant; what is important is that we provide the experience of using their own forms in genuinely user-type situations, constrained only by the limitations imposed by the institutional setting of school.

By such fluency work each student's level is self-monitoring, the relationship between content and form is natural, language must be used functionally, by definition, and an opportunity is provided for the linguistic items which have been offered through formal teaching or informal exposure to be brought to the surface and to enter the student's active system. Further, the strategies which are already possessed by all who can speak one language can be utilized for another. If (and it is not yet clear to what extent this is a major problem) the strategies used turn out to be inappropriate for English, then subsequent work can help to remedy the deficiency. But the emphasis is on what students can do rather than on what they cannot, and the language they use proceeds from their needs, wishes and interests as far as possible in the school situation.

Finally, and not the least important point, an emphasis on fluency does not require totally new materials, nor total retraining of teachers, nor a fundamentally new kind of syllabus. It extends tendencies which have always been present in sensitive teaching, and invokes procedures which many teachers have been using for many years. Since the basic emphasis is on methodology, any teacher can immediately move towards a more communicative teaching by a process of self-examination and self-consciousness in relation to teaching for accuracy and teaching for fluency.

Language, teaching and relationships

Teaching, I earlier maintained, is about relationships. So too, though in a different way, is much language use. The language teacher must necessarily be responsive to these claims—and of course it is awareness of this need that has led to a great deal of contemporary work on 'whole-person' teaching. The biggest risk in a 'scientific' account of language learning is that it claims objective value as a basis for teaching, and foreign and second language teaching has suffered particularly from lack of an educational perspective. The main difficulty is that description is not the same thing as performance. As teachers we are concerned with helping learning, not with describing what happens when we learn. Description of course has a value to us, but it is not the same thing as what we do. Helping someone requires a complex combination of abilities, perhaps too subtle for analysis, and certainly dependent on the personalities involved. I have used the analogy with marriage before, but it is not inapt—if not pressed too far. There are sociological observations to be made about marriage, and there are genuine pieces of advice to be given about probable successes and failures in marriage—but we do not choose who to marry on the basis of sociological studies or predictions. We cannot allow theorizing to become a substitute for the genuine relationship which develops between good teachers and their students, something which responds to the *particularities* of each situation, and not to the general trends which can be studied. A methodology of language teaching may be based on general principles, but any precise implementation of these principles must be the responsibility of the teacher and the students, for—because each human being is different—each class must be treated as a new group with needs and abilities which will never precisely reflect the needs and abilities of other groups. The teacher's responsibility is to develop a human relationship as fruitfully as possible, and to steer that relationship towards effective language learning. The successes of thousands of teachers show that this task, while demanding, is far from being impossible.

Teaching and research

Seeing teaching as part of human relationships had a number of important implications for the language teaching profession. One minor one, which it is worth referring to at the outset, is that it makes us question the value of a heavy emphasis on testing. There is a role for testing in any educational system, for some device is necessary to relate educational work with the requirements of society outside the school. But such a relationship can be accommodated within a fairly limited system of tests. The model which has most heavily influenced methodological development in recent years, however, has been one based on the empirical sciences in which experimental work has been carried out and has been evaluated in as formal a way as possible. This has a number of disadvantages for language teaching. One is that it tends to place great emphasis on the easily measurable formal patterns of the language at the expense of the less measurable ability to operate effectively. Even more important, it tends to devalue aspects of teaching which cannot be measurable because they are qualitative rather than quantitative and subjectively perceived rather than objectively. It is possible, indeed, that too much concern with easily measurable results, when we are dealing with a process which is complex, closely bound up with individual personalities, and long term, will damage the process of learning by its very presence. Language learning is certainly such a complex process. If its complexity means that typically learning is by slow accretion, with learners using different strategies at different times, operating different kinds of motivation at different times, and learning peripherally as well as centrally, holistically as well as sequentially, then the possibility of evaluating successful teaching in any simple way, even over the relatively short term, is greatly reduced. It may be worth asking ourselves how long a gap there may be between initial exposure to a particular linguistic item, and the ability to use it fluently—that is without thinking whenever the item is appropriate. Many textbooks, and a large number of tests, assume that use can follow teaching, sometimes in the same lesson, frequently in the same week. But, while it will differ considerably with different items, most teachers will agree that it is optimistic to expect real use of items 'taught' in less than six weeks or so, and often it will be substantially longer before items are fully internalized. And of course, even for native speakers there will be many linguistic items whose use is solely receptive. Even when fluency work enables students to use as fully as possible the systems of items they have learnt, the process of activation will be complicated and slow. Too much emphasis on pay-off through evaluation must be dangerous if we consider a model of language as a sequence of separable items as inappropriate.

There is a more important reason for considering teaching in its human aspects, and that is that it centres teaching on the classroom and the relationships that are found there. Now this is an area in which there can only be one expert: the teacher. Students are limited by only having had the experience of working as one person at language learning, while the teacher has had a close acquaintance with many learners. Researchers have studied and attempted to describe, but they have not, in their capacity as researchers, experienced directly the process of organizing and interacting with a class. Only the teacher has both breadth and depth of experience in using the relationship between themselves and their students to promote effective learning. Only they are in a position to understand their students with any appreciation of their full complexity as human beings. There is, as all teachers know, a 'feel', a 'gut response', an 'intuition' which cannot be gainsaid when something is working particularly well—that is when the relationship is both positive in human terms and productive in educational ones. Such intuitions are subjective and are consequently risky; they may be misplaced. But they are not necessarily misplaced, and they reflect—more than anything we can measure precisely—an important aspect of successful teaching.

The point of all this discussion is that teaching is an activity with an expertise of its own. It cannot be encompassed within an expertise of psychology or linguistics or sociology, and nor will the descriptive procedures appropriate for those or other disciplines be appropriate for the investigation of teaching. The shift in emphasis in language study referred to in this paper reflects an attempt to renew the connection between theoretical linguistics and language behaviour. Teaching, also, needs to look at its relationship with research. If language teaching and language use are really as complex as everyone seems to agree, the relationship between theory and the practice of teaching must also be complex and indirect. Teachers are expert in a process. Theorists have something to contribute to our understanding or that process, but only teachers experience it directly. One of the features of the past decade has been too heavy a reliance on untried, and often insensitive theorizing. What has been neglected is the relation with the practice of teaching. Any serious research programme for the next decade would do well to consider how sensitive, pragmatic responses to the need for language learning relate to current theories. We should, for example, look at the work of major writers like Harold Palmer, Michael West or Charles Fries in the light of our current preoccupations. We should, perhaps, reconsider some of the areas which have been for some time under a cloud. For example, if a notional syllabus is concerned with developing increasing sophistication with concepts, how does this relate to traditional concerns relating the teaching of language to the teaching of literature, or civilization? What role should methodological devices like the use of translation play? Should we look again at the use of bilingual dictionaries, or the uses of wordlists? Above all, should we look more carefully at the role played by successful language teachers (judged both in terms of results and on the subjective opinions of colleagues and students) in relation to communicative principles? Sometimes, as one studies research reports and theoretical discussion, it appears that we have had syllabus-centred study, materials-centred study, student-centred study, but—with one or two conspicuous exceptions—scarcely any teacher-centred study. Methodology has not eliminated the teacher variable, but it has successfully—or rather unsuccessfully— ignored it.

We cannot escape a relationship with research, as teachers. Indeed, serious research is essential for our continued improvement. But we must be informed by it, not dictated to, and more researchers need to understand teaching from the inside. The outlook is good, in some ways better now than it was ten years ago, for we are less dogmatic now, and better informed. But there are some worrying tendencies to look for new truths. We are often apparently searching for a proven firmer truth about teaching—a new humanism if not a new scientism. But the search is misplaced because that truth is not there. If teaching and language are about human relationships, then their processes will change as relationships change. There must be methodological principles, but they will be worked out in relation to individual classes and situations. In methodology, as in language, we must look for a process, not a product.

*   *   *   *   *

I have outlined a, perhaps somewhat sceptical, approach to the problems of teaching English to speakers of other languages. I hope that I have said things to which everyone here can react, in relation to their own personal teaching situation. My aim has been to open up questions to which we can return during the rest of this convention. In some ways we can look forward in confidence to the future, but with some suspicion of many current assumptions. Perhaps, if I have done nothing else, I have added another category of plenary talk: optimistical-cynical.

Some Current Problems in Communicative Language Teaching

(opening speech to the SPEAQ Convention, Quebec City, June 1982.
From the *SPEAQ Journal*, **6**, 1, 1982)

When I was invited to speak at this convention I was particularly asked to address myself to this topic. As a result, and in order to do it justice, I shall be summarizing some points which I have made elsewhere, as well as extending the argument in directions which seem particularly important from the perspective of Canada in 1982. What is certainly true at the moment is that methodologists feel rather like those little electric blobs in the middle of space invader games, threatened from all sides by instant extermination as they are pulled in one direction by the demands for practical and immediate solutions to problems by the teaching profession, and assailed from the other by new communicative and humanistic proposals by applied linguists, materials developers and syllabus designers, or destroyers.

I propose, though, to speak about communicative teaching, without assuming that that will necessarily be functional-notional teaching, and to move from three base points to a teaching view of the learning process. I say a 'teaching' view because we are here at this convention in our capacities as teachers, because we are paid for what we do as teachers, and because any intervention we make in the activities of our students is made as a teacher. Consequently, however important it is for us to understand learners and learning, it is also important for us to understand the position from which we act professionally, and how it differs from that of the learner. I shall be moving, that is to say, towards a view of teaching methodology, not to a view of the language learning process or of the description of language, or classrooms, or communication.

Because of this, I want to concentrate on being realistic—which means that what I have to say must be interpretable for normal schools as they have to operate in the world as it is, that I must make no claims which cannot be justified by our experience and intuitions about normal classroom possibilities, and that what I say must be perceived as comprehensible and relevant by normal classroom teachers— not only by the committed and excited who read journals, come to SPEAQ Conventions or only live for their profession. This may sound as if I am determined to fight with my hands tied behind my back, and indeed it will lead to some caution over the more extravagant possible statements, but there are good reasons for adopting this position. For one thing, innovations which only appeal to the most dedicated in the profession will probably only affect the most dedicated, and they are by definition a small minority; but more important, it is only the great mass of the teaching profession which can validate, by close contact day after day with typical classes, the speculations of those who think, write and speak from outside the classroom. It is sometimes helpful, with teaching methods as with language, to isolate the discussion from specific social situations, but proposals for effective teaching must rely heavily on feedback mechanisms which can only come from typical students in typical schools with typical teachers.

Nor will this orientation lead simply to caution and care. It may lead to something which is, in the present atmosphere, rather daring: the recognition of teachers' professional expertise, derived from experience and tradition, as being a major contribution to our understanding of teaching, and not something to be seen merely as a reactionary impediment to innovation and creative thinking. We need teachers' experience and intuition, so long as it is allied with knowledge of possible options and contact with imaginative research. Any successful innovation must depend on a combination of all these.

Let me now consider the three base points for our discussion of language teaching.

Base Point One. We know less than we would like to about language and language learning

If we were researchers, this fact should spur us to more creative hypothesis formation and consequent testing. But the purpose of language teaching is not to *understand* language and language learning, but to produce effective acquisition in others. Such understanding as we have of the processes of language learning must feed in to our professional activities, but we must recognize that people have taught languages, and learnt them, very effectively without having much understanding at all of how they are learnt, or by operating with extremely bizarre ideas about the processes involved (I met a very competent English speaker once who swore that the only formal learning she had done was reading the novels of George Eliot, unsimplified, with the aid of a dictionary.) Just to give an illustration of what I mean by our lack of knowledge, let me instance a typical report of a research seminar. Last September the British Association for Applied Linguistics held a seminar on interpretative strategies in language learning—a central issue to communicative teaching—and isolated the following problems in the organizers' report: the differences between the ways in which researchers defined 'strategies'; how to distinguish interpretation and learning strategies; how to infer mental strategies from overt behaviour; and the need for a more integrated theory (*BAAL Newsletter*, No. 14, Spring 1982). The point about this is that it is typical—which is not to make any kind of criticism of research or researchers, but simply to draw attention to the constantly changing nature of our understanding of psychology, linguistics, the educational process, and so on. Teaching continues, but we cannot claim that it is in some sense a translation of our understanding of language learning, for its dynamic is a product of the process of interaction between teachers, students, institutions and the demands of society. My conclusions from Base Point One, then, are:

1. We cannot say with confidence that we know exactly how language is learnt, and we cannot rely on the expertise that derives from the potentially contributory disciplines, so
2. We cannot legitimately force teachers or students to follow a particular procedure on the basis of these disciplines as we lack sufficient authority in our understanding to be so intolerant.

Base Point Two. Teaching is not the obverse of learning

This is a point that I have argued more fully elsewhere (Brumfit, 1984), and for an interesting semantic analysis of the various possible relationships (based on the sentence 'The teacher taught the student English': see Halliday, 1976). Apart from the fundamental difference that teaching is causative in intention, while learning is not, most of the differences proceed from the point that teaching is overt and visible, while learning is covert and hidden. Thus, teaching takes place in real time, and therefore in a linear fashion; it can therefore be planned; it is the product of conscious decision-making and effort, and therefore can be based on a syllabus; we can test whether the appropriate actions are being performed, and thus produce 'professionals'; these actions can be administratively interfered with; and its effectiveness cannot be measured—because we can never know in normal situations whether it was the teaching or something else that caused the changes in the learner. In contrast, learning may occur willingly or unwillingly; it may be linear but it may happen in an instantaneous flash of inspiration; it cannot usually be planned; it is often not the immediate result of conscious effort (how often do we complain, 'The more I try the less I learn'?); it cannot be reliably based on a syllabus; the results can be tested, but not the process; learners do not constitute a profession; they are not administratively constrained; and the effectiveness of learning can be measured—by its results. This is a somewhat condensed account of a complicated series of distinctions, but the basic point should be clear. We can talk about teaching with some precision, because we can watch teaching happening— but we cannot, except with excessively over-simple models, watch learning happening at all. (None of this is to deny that learning may be influenced by accidental and casual encounters with teachers or others; however, teaching normally is a deliberate, and therefore self-aware attempt on the part of someone to cause learning to take place in someone else.) Teaching is thus about making learning available, while learning is about successfully changing one's own behaviour. From a consideration of Base Point Two I conclude:

1. We can control teaching; we cannot control learning.
2. Therefore, we should not be ashamed of talking about teaching as a different phenomenon from learning.
3. We cannot specify the relationships between teachers and learners as being a simple matter of input, leading to output.

I would also, before moving on to the final base point, like to draw attention to one kind of understanding of teaching which can easily be neglected in the analysis of classrooms: direct participatory experience. Many social scientists have discussed the role of experience, and Winch has put the issue well:

> . . . a historian or sociologist of religion must himself have some religious feeling if he is to make sense of the religious movement he is studying and understand the considerations which govern the lives of its participants. A historian of art must have some aesthetic sense if he is to understand the problems confronting the artists of his period; and without this he will have left out of his account precisely what would have made it a history of *art*, as opposed to a rather puzzling external account of certain motions which certain people have been perceived to go through. (Winch, 1958: 88)

'Talking about teaching' must take into account that pedagogic feeling which can only derive from extensive experience of teaching.

Base Point Three. Language use is dynamic, not static

There has been a shift in our attitude to language in the last fifteen years or so which could constitute a genuine paradigm shift for language teaching. I do not need to spell it out in detail: those interested can pursue the discussion, in ascending order of difficulty, in Johnson and Morrow, 1981; Brumfit, 1980, Part Two; Widdowson, 1978; Johnson, 1982; Brumfit and Johnson, 1979; Canale and Swain, 1980; Widdowson, 1979. The basic argument is that people do not *possess* language, they *use* it. Philosophers like Grice (1975) and social psychologists like Giles (1977) have suggested or observed some of the ways in which we do this. Sociolinguists like Labov (1972) have indicated how language varies in relation to social context. Linguists like Halliday (1973) have examined ways in which language structure and language function are interrelated. And language teaching theorists like van Ek (1975), Wilkins (1976) and Widdowson (1978) have attempted to incorporate many of these insights into specifications for syllabuses or materials. Essentially, language is seen as the creation of meaning by negotiation between speakers, or readers and writers. No two people will speak exactly the same dialect, but they will normally co-operate together to establish their purposes, the meanings of the language they use in relation to those purposes, and the amount of knowledge they share to enable them to achieve the purposes. They will communicate in this way by using the communication tokens that they share—linguistic and non-linguistic—and these tokens will clearly be more efficient when they are close to each other, that is when people speak similar dialects. There will also be fairly clearly established routines for performing common tasks of communication, so that negotiation is less between those who know each other well, or in stereotyped situations where the needs are highly predictable. Learning to mean, or learning to negotiate, is therefore not simply a matter of learning the tokens of the language, but how to use them as well. In some ways it is analogous to activities like swimming or driving, where the basic information for instruction is fairly simple, but a great deal of practice is necessary in interacting with water or traffic before we can be said to have learnt successfully. (And note that functional analyses are possible of both swimming and driving, but we do not use them in teaching the basic skills: what we do is provide a supportive environment and plenty of practice in situations which are less demanding than rough seas or rush-hour traffic.) From this view of the nature of language I conclude:

1. We are teaching people to *do* something, not to describe or understand it (this is of course a favourite audiolingual premiss).
2. Comparisons with, for example, music are only partially valid—drilled routines may have a place, but language is essentially an interaction with other people who are themselves interacting and it is more like learning to play duets than learning to play the piano.
3. Using language must necessitate negotiating agreed cultural values (a point I shall expand on in a moment) since language interacts with cultural meaning.

4. Hence, the teacher can only provide the tokens of the language, but the learners themselves must experience and create the process of negotiation and value-creation.

Discussion

Let me illustrate the basic problem with a metaphor. When we go to a new country we have to use a new currency. We can easily learn the basic tokens of the currency—the number of cents in a dollar, colloquial terms like 'dime', 'quarter' and 'nickel', the sizes of coins and the denominations of the notes. But knowing these does not enable us to operate the currency satisfactorily. To do this we have to achieve some sense of the values of the foreign culture—which goods are scarce, which goods are highly prized, what their role is in the culture. And this is not simply a matter of translation. Wine in a wine-drinking culture has a different price from wine in Britain, and also means perhaps a different quality of product when it is freely available—in some ways its value equivalent in Britain may be milk, though not exactly. The point is that to operate the currency of the foreign country we need a vast range of subtle intuitions so that we know at once whether the price asked is high or low, so that we can feel instinctively for a small ten-cent piece rather than a large five-cent one, so that we can immediately react to prices without always translating back into our home currency. I do not know in Canada whether five dollars is amazingly good value for a student concert, or expensive, and I cannot fluently operate the Canadian currency until I have acquired a vast range of intuitions which can only be obtained through experience of spending money in Canada. *But*, I can bring to Canada experience of spending money, flexibly, in a range of other cultural settings, so that I am attuned to the possible risks and problems, and I could have had some simulated exchange activity before I came if the situation had been even more complicated (as it is with language) and my needs great enough.

The point I want to stress here is that language teaching traditionally has concerned itself solely or largely with teaching about the tokens of negotiation. This is a necessary preliminary to learning to negotiate, and it is of course the area where the teacher has most to contribute as teacher, for the teacher can give students access to the tokens of negotiation through the materials chosen, the syllabus organization and the much discussed and trained techniques of presentation and practice. But these techniques, together with the correction processes initiated by teachers, always rely on our knowledge of the idealized, static system of the language. To respond to the learner's need to experience language use we must develop techniques out of our experience of groupwork, game-playing, role play and simulation activities, extensive reading and even creative writing in order to offer students the chance to say what they have not been explicitly taught to say, to express meanings that they have chosen themselves, and to adjust and adapt their language to that of those with whom they communicate. None of these processes is completely new to language teaching, so what is demanded is in no sense a major break with the traditions of the past, but it is important to emphasize that such activities must become central to language teaching, and not simply peripheral.

There is another reason for wanting classroom activity to be based on student needs for a substantial part of the time. This relates to my Base Point One. We know that people do learn languages, and we often, through our interaction with them as teachers, help them to do it. But the more we give them chances of using their own language in the performance of tasks which have been specified as lightly as possible by the teacher (always with the recognition that they must be tasks that they can at least begin to perform in the target language), the more likely they are to use their own level of language, rather than a hypothetical level we have decided ourselves to be appropriate for them, and the more likely they are to adopt strategies that feel comfortable and appropriate for them on the basis of their own experience. A tight hand by the teacher implies that we know how learners should learn. Often we do not, so a loose hand seems preferable.

We have a position, then, in which the teacher teaches the tokens of the language—that is, makes available to students the formal, basic patterns of grammar and pronunciation, as well as important vocabulary items—perhaps by very traditional means. But this is only the preliminary move in the process of learning. The teacher must also allow students to assist their own process of internalization by using the language as fluently as possible, that is by behaving with the inadequate English they have so far developed in the same way as they behave in mother tongue. Extensive reading, natural writing exercises, extensive listening, and natural conversation, all in formally inadequate English, will be necessary to assist this process. And while the teacher will correct on some occasions, for much of the fluency activity when the language is being used naturally, the teacher will only respond as a communicator, so that students have the chance to become autonomous users of such language as they have acquired. In this way a developing and negotiating, dynamic system is being used, and not a static one based on the alien knowledge of the textbook or teacher.

The relationship that the teacher has built with the class will thus become a crucial factor in the development of language use. But the techniques will be techniques which have a long history in language teaching, and the skills demanded of teachers will be the basic interaction skills that they have always been concerned to develop.

How, then does functional-notional discussion fit in to all this? First, it is important to say that communicative teaching *can* be based on grammatical, or any other kind of syllabus, providing the syllabus is not seen as a specification of everything that happens in class. The chance to perform communicatively, for example by small group discussion, in English, of the answers to traditional textbook exercises, is available to any class with any materials or type of syllabus. Similarly, it is perfectly possible to envisage a functional syllabus being taught uncommunicatively—if, for example, the teacher teaches all about possible functions and their realizations without providing either practice or the chance to experiment or use language uncontrolledly. Without a methodology that converts the static syllabus listings into dynamic language activity no syllabus can become communicative.

But a functional-notional syllabus does demand that teachers become sensitive to the range of possible things to be done in English, with the possible settings in which students could use language, and the general constellations of meaning that may be required of them. Thus such a syllabus may help teachers in the choice of language activities to direct their work more precisely towards use, and may act as a check list so that they can ensure that all major areas of language use have been covered. A grammatical syllabus can do none of these things in itself. However, if we join the experience of sophisticated users of grammatical syllabuses to the structure of functional-notional ones we shall arrive at a methodological solution to the dynamic needs of learners. Good teachers have always tried to make grammatical syllabuses dynamic. A functional syllabus is another tool for assisting this process. In addition to the procedures already referred to, techniques such as those in Maley and Duff (1978), Moskowitz (1978) and Ur (1981) will be useful. But in the last resort, we must rely on our accumulated experience and expertise as teachers.

To summarize: being communicative is as much or more a matter of methodology as of syllabus or materials, and methodology is something that teachers are uniquely qualified to contribute to. We should therefore be willing to use our expertise, to innovate, to improve, to inform each other, and to criticize. In this sphere we are experts insofar as we are teachers. The President of SPEAQ, in her opening remarks, told us that 'to communicate is the beginning of understanding'. There is wisdom in recognizing that it is the beginning, the beginning of a language process that we can start but cannot finish. As teachers we can set people off on the track of language extension and development, but we have to allow them to continue the process themselves.

Section Two:

THE CONTEXT OF LANGUAGE TEACHING

These three papers are all attempts to contextualize language teaching in a broader view than that of teaching technique. The first paper considers the nature of 'English' when it is talked about, as it so often is, as an international language, and discusses the various ways in which that term can be understood. The second examines the bases of applied linguistics and the theoretical view of language that distinguishes applied from pure linguistics. This inevitably leads on to consideration of various methodological issues for applied linguistic research and discussion. The third paper examines approaches to language teaching across the educational spectrum, including mother tongue, second language, and foreign language work.

All these papers, in their different ways, are trying to take us beyond the narrow categories within which we customarily view our responsibilities, and trying to establish appropriate connections wherever these seem to be helpful.

'English as an International Language': what do we mean by 'English'?

(adapted from a paper in *English for International Communication*, Ed. C. J. Brumfit, Pergamon, 1982)

It is the purpose of this paper to consider what kind of a claim we are making when we talk loosely about English as an international language. The phrase conceals a number of possible claims, and it is worthwhile for us to disentangle them as far as possible if we are to distinguish between different types of argument.

First of all it is quite clear that as a statement of simple fact English *is* an international language in that it is the most widespread medium of international communication, both because of the number and geographical spread of its speakers, and because of the large number of non-native speakers who use it for part at least of their international contact. The predominance of English is mainly the result of two periods of world domination by English-speaking countries: British imperialism in the nineteenth century, and the economic influence of the United States in the twentieth century. The combination of political influence and technological superiority acquired through these two successive movements has given English an advantage over other major imperial languages such as French or Spanish, while the relative geographical restrictions of Russian, Chinese in its many forms or Arabic have made these languages less influential internationally. It should be noted, though, that this manifest international success has inevitably been bought at some cost. A language which can be identified with the largest nineteenth-century imperial power or with the greatest capitalist power of the twentieth century will inevitably be perceived as an instrument of cultural and ideological domination in parts of the world where the language situation is unstable enough to demand debate. In many places, including India, many parts of Africa, France, Italy and Latin America, the role of English has come under strong attack within the last twenty years.

Yet we need to be clear what the choices are. There is a naive view of linguistic imperialism which argues that people have a right to be brought up in their own culture with their own language, and that outsiders should defend this right because of the evil effects of external domination. This view, which does have the virtue of recognizing the genuine threat implicit in external linguistic domination, nonetheless fails to recognize the complexity and power of the forces towards communication on a larger and larger scale. Isolation is impossible, and for many peoples the choice is between communication or exploitation. Possession of any language leads us to communicate with groups other than our own, and as the world becomes more and more interconnected by trade, improved communications, medical, political and cultural demands, the need for communication—as a way of enabling people to control and influence their own destinies—will inevitably increase. This will not necessarily lead to the emergence of *one* world language, but it must produce a

35

demand for one or more auxiliary languages to complement those with only local currency. It is true that decisions about which languages should be promoted for national and international communication necessarily have to be sensitive to political, economic and ideological implications, but the only way in which contact with some major language can be avoided—for representatives of most groups of people in the world—is by remaining an isolated, ghettoized culture. Such a culture will either lose the benefits of wider economic and political contact altogether, or will be at the mercy of decisions made outside in which members of the minority group will have no voice.

It is often claimed, however, that in some sense English is peculiarly suited to be an international language. Such a claim may entail a number of different propositions, some of which follow from the present international status of English and some of which do not. It may be claimed, for example, that in some way the structure of English is peculiarly adapted for international communication, or that English is phonologically more accessible to most learners than other languages are. These are, it is true, questions of greater theoretical interest now than they were a few years ago. In linguistics it has normally been accepted as axiomatic that different languages are equally easy (or difficult) for native speakers to learn. However, it is important to recognize that this is a procedural axiom which is dependent on a view of all languages as developed and equally complex. A notion of differential competence among language users, which has become an increasingly interesting focus of investigation in the past decade, does allow us—at least in principle—to conceive of groups of language users whose language is relatively more simple than that of other groups. And further, if the acquisition of language is closely bound up with the uses to which it is put—that is, if the language structure acquired is a consequence of the functional load placed on it while it is being learnt—then a language responding to varied and diverse functional needs should in principle become in some sense richer than one which responds to a more limited set of functional demands. The increasing concern with language variation of recent years makes it possible to discuss such hypotheses without questioning the foundations on which descriptive linguistics rests.

But such discussion, while interesting to pursue, is still hypothetical. Nor do such arguments require that an internationally-used language should be more complex in structure than one used within one homogeneous culture. Functional variation and sensitivity may be achieved through increased vocabulary and an insistence on the public maintenance of fine distinctions of meaning. Any language is capable of enormous variation within its basic structure by the creation or borrowing of new words, and by a socially accepted concern for precision, rather than the tolerant vagueness of meaning characteristic of much casual speech. One language may be effective in far more spheres than another simply by virtue of a larger vocabulary and the social attitudes of its users. And it is social attitudes, also, which will influence the ease with which pronunciation can be learnt. There is probably more tolerance now of foreigner pronunciation than there was even a decade ago, as a result of our recognition that phonology is more negotiable than syntax in normal discourse. There seems to be little evidence that any language provides an overwhelming barrier phonologically if the social motivation for learning is provided by political or economic demands.

There are, however, two other types of claim which might be made for English. It might be claimed that the lexicon of English is peculiarly suited to international communication, or that it is in discourse terms well adjusted to the requirements of different culture. Neither of these claims is especially interesting theoretically; indeed they may simply be tantological on the claim that English is used internationally. The vocabulary of a language will expand, infinitely in principle, depending on the demands which are made on it, and any language carries within it the capacity to be modified to the demands of particular types of discourse. English may have been fortunate in its past, from these points of view, but that implies no virtue for its future.

The same claim might be extended beyond the language to its users. It is a possibility that speakers of English are more tolerant of foreigner talk than speakers of some other languages. It may even be possible that such speakers are more tolerant of lexical innovation than others. But such characteristics cannot be attributed to the language itself: they are more likely to be features of a culture which may coincide to a large extent, but which cannot be coextensive with speakers of the language. Only a strong Whorfian position would allow us to relate directly from language to users in this way. Anyway, it is perfectly possible to conceive of a political reaction to the overseas use of English which would lead to a much greater movement towards intolerance and a consequent restriction on native speaker acceptance of deviation. We might then wish to claim that the process of internationalization has gone too far to be halted, and that English is no longer the possession of native speakers, but this, again, is simply an inevitable consequence of the statement that English is *de facto* an international language.

So far it has been argued that claims about the suitability of English to be an international language on the grounds of its internal characteristics are consequences of its international status rather than causes; they are all in essence tautological. Another claim which could be made also reflects the accidental fact of its world dominance, but has more interesting repercussions for discussion of the future. We may concede that there is nothing intrinsic to English as a language which makes it qualified for international status, but still point to the widely attested fact of the world demand for the language as an illustration of the motivation to learn it, which makes it more likely that it can successfully achieve a firm international base and remain unrivalled. Certainly, the motivation to learn English exists, to the pleasure of teachers of English overseas—as with North Sea oil, from no merit of our own we find we are living on a rich commercial asset, providing we do not fritter it away by economic mismanagement—but it is a motivation which could of course disappear if the political and economic circumstances changed. The motivation is dependent on the learner vision of themselves as members of a more-or-less English using culture, at least for some purposes, and a culture which is highly valued to justify the effort, time and money to be expended on learning English rather than doing more attractive things. Consequently, any discussion of the use of English for international purposes must eventually come to consider how to make teaching easier, quicker and cheaper. The large-scale motivation can only be a response to the larger historical movements which are outside individual control, but the other side of the equation, attitudes to teaching, can be confronted more directly.

Much discussion of teaching is essentially concerned with problems of simplification, an interest with a long and honourable pedigree in English language teaching. For many years vocabulary simplification and grading has been investigated and practised by teachers and researchers in written materials and by teachers as they improvized in the classroom. More recent work, though possibly pedagogically less well-founded, has concentrated on structural simplification. And teachers through their classroom methodology have practised grading in discourse terms (and indeed phonologically) long before such procedures were described by linguists and classroom researchers. At the same time there have been several attempts to achieve simple systems for the learning of English (Basic English being perhaps the most famous) both within and without the formal educational systems. Throughout the past century there have been successions of successful 'methods', usually combining simplification procedures, of variable sophistication, with methodological innovations and skilful marketing. Some of these have even been taken up by parliamentarians as answers to the perennial problems of language learning.

Discussion of simplification has often been confused, however, for there seem to be two separable issues at stake. Not everyone who wants to learn 'English' is actually after a fully-fledged language, at least in the first instance. Many professions need basic communication systems, which use English words and even basic English structure, to provide a simple and accessible code. The languages of the sea or of air traffic control, fit into this category. In many ways the use of English tokens for this limited use of language is fortuitous. Although the language used may allow very limited negotiation, it is not very different from the perfectly recited descriptions of exhibits at the Shanghai Trade Fair which used to be provided by Chinese guides who could not answer a single question when asked. The characteristic of a language is not its formal features but its ability to be used for the negotiation of meaning. Some simple languages need to be only minimally negotiable (indeed they may prove literally disastrous if they are open to negotiation, as with air traffic controllers), but for this reason their relation with genuine language is slight. They are necessary, but they should not be confused with the languages which do require full human participation. To learn the latter requires at least three conditions to be fulfilled:

(a) there must be extensive exposure (some would say systematic exposure) to the target language;
(b) there must be extensive opportunity to use the language so far acquired as creatively as possible—through reading, writing, conversation, listening activities, whichever are most appropriate to particular learners;
(c) students must be motivated to benefit from (a) and (b).

It is unclear whether teachers can do very much about (c) except in a limited way by the efficiency and excitement of their work. But (a) and (b) are, of course, within the teacher's control. One of the issues which is by no means clearly resolved is the nature of the exposure to the target language. There are those who argue that we should attempt to teach something which is a simplified version of English, that the target for the non-native speaker should be different from the native-speaker model. This claim can be interpreted in two ways. We may say as a matter of fact that non-native speakers do not become indistinguishable from native speakers so that we should recognize this in expecting them to attain simply to the standards of the best speakers from their linguistic group. (In practice this usually means being markedly deviant in accent, perhaps slightly deviant in spoken syntax, and scarcely deviant at all in writing except where cultural variation demands unEnglish forms in order to express a foreign culture.) This position, paradoxically, involves recognizing the non-native speaker as equivalent to the native, for native speakers too reveal their origins in accent, deviate in spoken syntax, and only vary in writing where there are significant cultural differences to express. The second interpretation is that we can specify a simpler form of English which is peculiarly suitable for international use. Here the crucial issue is whether we want the simple form to be learner created or teacher (or materials writer) dictated. There is plenty of evidence that learners create their own simple systems out of the English to which they are exposed, and that they fossilize at levels of attainment below those demanded by examinations or employers (though, of course, many learners continue to develop until they become indistinguishable from native speakers except in accent). Whether or not there is a strong case for deliberately creating a special language for students to learn presumably depends on the claims that such a language will in fact be easier to learn and teach, and that such a language will be able to perform adequately in interaction with the English being produced in return—that it possesses the essential negotiating capacity of a naturally usable language. Since it is difficult to imagine a situation where such a simple language will be used to converse solely with other users of the simple language (for insofar as it is used naturally it will expand naturally and will stop being simple), it is likely that the simple language will eventually be required as no more than a source for comprehension of natural English. In other words the simple language must in the long run be seen as a pedagogic device in relation to learning normal English, not as a substitute for normal English. The problems of creating a culture of Basic English users, Esperanto users or of users of any other artificially created language are insuperable. But the value of a language which assists the process of language acquisition so that learners can exploit their own capacities most effectively will be enormous.

At the same time, though, there will be a curious relationship between any simple, pedagogical language and natural culture. The process of live language use which is increasingly being seen as necessary for language acquisition as well as language maintenance depends on the language, whether native or foreign, expressing a living culture. Consequently, while it is possible to maintain that in principle the teaching of a language is teaching a tool for use with no ideological or social implications, the successful take-up of this teaching must depend on learners integrating the language with their own ideological and social needs. The extent to which teachers need actively to assist this process has been a matter for debate for some time. It is true that, in the context of highly specialized ESP groups, the cultural and social context may be well defined in relation to particular technical and scientific needs, but these nonetheless constitute a culture, and even ESP language work normally spills over into wider concerns as soon as it is fully taken over by students, for it is rare for language users to achieve total separation between the various social roles that they play. The stronger the movement towards a functional view of language teaching, the greater the necessity for it to be seen as co-ordinated with the social, political, economic, even ethical and religious needs of learners.

All this leads to a curious paradox. There is a strong movement throughout the world towards greater communication across cultures, and the English language cannot avoid having a major role to play in this process. This is a sociological fact. But there are risks as well as advantages in this process for the native-speaking English countries. On the one hand we shall benefit culturally in many ways by having direct access to cultures which are historically and geographically far away from ourselves as English is used for secondary purposes by more and more people outside our traditional spheres of influence. And we shall no doubt achieve economic, even perhaps some political advantages, by sharing a common language. But we risk also creating enmities as well as loyalties. There is already evidence that the varied sources of English are being exploited by countries in their attitudes to learning English. American English may be preferred to British by countries wishing to express their independence from a traditional British connection; countries too closely connected by geography or history to the States have been known to turn towards Britain for a change in model and teaching policy for their English. The same is happening in contacts with Australia and New Zealand. The English-speaking world can be played politically by the non-English-speaking world. Nor need this process be seen solely between the varieties of the English language. At the beginning of this paper it was argued that the world must have international languages—but there is no necessity for there to be only one. People, and nations, need to be able to hide behind misunderstanding as well as reveal all to each other. The world, unless it manifests an unprecedented desire for unity in the near future, will require a minimum of two international languages, if only to play them off against each other in self-defence. The paradox for the development of English as an international language is that the more multicultured English becomes the more it will be perceived as a threat and the more it will, in the end, lead people to wish for some alternatives to English. In the meantime, however, users of the English language have been provided with a unique opportunity for cross-cultural contact on a hitherto unprecedented scale. The immediate gains will be not merely political and economic, but linguistic and pedagogic also, as we understand more fully the process of linguistic adaptation to the widely varied needs of people throughout the world. But we do need to consider the paradox very carefully. Perhaps those who care for international communication and world peace should put their efforts into ensuring that there are several viable languages of international communication, and should resist pressures for a whole world of second-language English users.

Being Interdisciplinary: problems in defining applied linguistics

(originally presented as a paper to the BAAL Annual General Meeting in Manchester, September 1979. Slightly modified from the version published in *Applied Linguistics*, **1**, 2, 1980)

In this paper I hope to consider a problem which faces any applied activity—that of relating insights drawn from a variety of different disciplines to the solution of specific practical difficulties.

This problem is particularly acute for applied linguistics, for language problems are by their nature complex and intimately bound up with human needs and behaviour. Any abstraction or idealization of linguistic performance which may be methodologically necessary for the descriptive linguist (Lyons, 1972) has to be confused by social and psychological factors as soon as the connection is renewed, as it must be as soon as we consider classrooms, or literary traditions, or medical services. There have of course been attempts to incorporate linguistic procedures into teaching in fairly undiluted forms, but even when textbooks demonstrate a close relation between theoretical assumptions and classroom practice (e.g. in very different ways, Kennedy, 1930, and Roberts, 1964), the intervention of the teacher will certainly reflect pedagogic as much as descriptive requirements. And, of course, educationists are always ready to complain that the concerns of theorists have too little to say for teachers (Rosen, 1978).

The difficulty arises partly because language is simultaneously used to express what Halliday (1975) has called 'mathetic' acts of meaning ('an act of meaning that is self-sufficient, calls for no response, and functions as an explicit reality-creating device': Halliday, 1979, p.83), and pragmatic acts which are essentially interactional. There is thus a conceptual dimension to be explored as well as one incorporating strategies for social interaction. However, the complexity and availability of language poses its own problems, for the system can be isolated and idealized to give rise to complex and fascinating analysis and speculation—witness the whole history of linguistics itself. Language is thus a system which is operated and negotiated socially, a system which enables individuals to comprehend and classify their own experience, and a system which is capable of being abstracted, reified and examined in isolation from both individuals and society. The first two systems interact, to increase the complication, and furthermore carry tremendous extra weight, for the social-linguistic system operates, by definition, cross-culturally, involving structures of meaning which have scarcely yet been explored in which we ourselves participate and which we cannot therefore objectify (see, for example, Bernstein, 1975), and the psycholinguistic system, both in learning and use, involves considerations of motivation and cognitive depth (see Stevick, 1976) as well as the whole weight of individual past experience. Yet these two systems are the material we actually work with, while the last is no more than a methodological device—albeit a necessary one—to enable us to come to grips with the other two systems.

Language is not of course the only system of interaction, nor the only symbolic system, but with no other systems is the power to generate complex and subtle symbols so closely related to the specifiable features of the interactive process: our idealized linguistic system appears to give us a metalanguage to explore the means of communication and conceptualization.

Stated like this, it might appear that the suspicion of linguistics shown by psychologists and sociologists in the past had good reason. A major contribution of linguistics, however, has been to demonstrate the complexity of the language process. The linguistic system, even in an idealized and standardized form, defies simple explanation, and tendencies to oversimplify result in apparently naive discussion of the role of language in society or in learning processes. The most widespread naivety in this direction centres on the relationship between language use and the concepts associated with particular examples of usage. Much discussion of Bernstein's early work (1971), adequately criticized by Stubbs (1976), Trudgill (1975) and Rogers (1976), assumed a close and clearly specifiable relationship between language and concept formation, and such a relationship is assumed by many—perhaps most—sociologists when writing about language. It is also implicit, of course, in the discussion of language associated with sexist and racist attitudes. The difficulty is that meaning is both conventional and arbitrary. The descriptive terms of one decade may be the insults of another ('negro', 'fascist'), but there is always an element of human intention—we are not the prisoners of our own semiotic system—unless, that is, enough of us choose to be and thus change the convention. When someone says 'The sun rises in the east', he does not demonstrate himself to believe in a pre-Copernican universe, and I have not demonstrated myself by my use of 'he' and 'himself' in this sentence to be a believer in an all-male human race—but the two cases are distinct nonetheless, for the sexist issue is live where the other is dead and we can only speak effectively the language of those we speak to.

It may be true that sociologists have frequently written as if language determined reality, to the posthumous delight of Whorf, and it may also be true that psychologists have seen language as primarily about naming, at least until fairly recently. Such differences in attitude may have been partially responsible for the greater enthusiasm with which psychologists regarded the linguistic advances of the various apes who have been taught 'language' (Linden, 1975). What about the linguists themselves, however? How has their view of language been partial? Certainly, over-emphasis on the centrality of syntax can lead to a distorted view of language work in schools, particularly if such a view is coupled with a learning theory which ignores cognitive and contextual requirements (Stevick, 1976). The greatest risk lies more in the confusion of procedures which are in essence investigatory and descriptive with those that are developmental and pedagogical. Attempts to develop a particular person's ability in a language demand quite separate procedures from attempts to develop the understanding of the human race about the nature of language, or indeed the nature of a particular language. The former is intrinsically a subjective operation, the latter an objective one, for the former can be judged by results without reference to the means—which may be hidden—and with the latter the means, the explicitness of the procedures used, *is* the process. The goal for language learners is determined by the conditions for effective operation in the community of language users to which they aspire. The goal for scholars cannot be this, since the 'truth' cannot be final. They can hope for no more than to present an approach so clearly that the criticisms made of that approach lead to further and better analyses, and improved explanatory models.

Now the differences in attitude to language reflect primarily the differing interests of the practitioners of the various disciplines. This is obvious. But the person who applied insights to a particular problem has to operate in a world where the differing concerns of different disciplines become confusing. Language, as was pointed out above, operates simultaneously in several directions at once: the network is so intricate that no one variable can be held constant without many others being distorted. In cases of severe malfunction drastic actions (i.e. those based on a grossly over-simplified view of the working of language) may be necessary. But most applications of linguistic insights are concerned not with severe malfunction but with absolutely normal situations. This is true particularly of the application of linguistics to language teaching. Applications to language teaching of views of language restricted to any one discipline will be inappropriate in that they will limit language to too restricted a set of features. Language cannot be seen purely as a creator of ideology because we can break its meaning if we choose to; it cannot be seen solely as a device for establishing categories or merely as exemplifications of particular syntactic patterns because in the former case language in use characteristically does other things as well or because in the latter case we are not primarily teaching the process of linguistic description. An over-emphasis on language for 'making sense of the world' may lead to too insensitive an emphasis on creative writing at the expense of working towards social norms which have to be recognized for effective communication to occur, or on the mathetic at the expense of the pragmatic. An over-emphasis on the pragmatic for foreign learners may lead to neglect of mathetic aspects essential for genuine internalization.

But we are remaining at the moment the prisoner of our own categorizations. The dimensions of language we want to explore can be readily fitted in to the patterns of the various intellectual disciplines, since we recognize the boundaries imposed by these disciplines. In what sense can problems of application be similarly fitted in to discipline boundaries? In practice, we expect our students to look at the linguistic environment variously from sociological, psychological, or pedagogic points of view and to marry together their conclusions as best they can. Readers on applied linguistics and introductory language teaching books (Wilkins, 1972a; Allen and Corder, 1973; Corder, 1973) no less than books on language for all teachers (Wilkinson, 1971, 1975) put together information drawn from research sources in various disciplines as if there is no problem of compatibility. And, indeed, while talking loosely and suggestively about the solution of practical difficulties there is very little problem. The big difficulty arises when we want to ask that applied linguistics should justify itself as a term by showing itself to be something other than discussion of practical problems encountered in (mainly) language teaching. It has, indeed, been suggested recently by Bernard Spolsky that it would be more appropriate to use the term 'educational linguistics', by analogy with educational psychology or educational philosophy for the application of linguistic insights to teaching problems (Spolsky, 1978). And there is no doubt that a great deal remains to be learnt from linguists, in various forms, working in education.

Part of this discussion appears to lead to an argument about terminology which it would be easy to trivialize. Put at its starkest, if applied linguistics were to be considered *merely* the application of linguistics to anything to which it could be applied, then it would be no more than a mirror for linguists to peer into—for the only issues which linguistics can confront alone are linguistic issues, not applied ones. If real problems are to be confronted, as was argued above, the issues will not be solely linguistic. Whether we call the intelligent solution of problems in which language plays a major part, applied linguistics or not is not important, providing the use of the term does not obscure important truths about the activity.

However, the argument about terminology may conceal a more fundamental difficulty, revealed not in the connection with linguistics, but in the formality of the term 'applied linguistics'. Pit Corder asks pertinently, 'Can we say that any of the approaches to language as knowledge, as behaviour, as skill, as habit, as an event or an object can safely be disregarded by the language teacher?' (Corder, 1973, p.21). Yet by using the term 'applied linguistics' we imply that there is something, some procedure perhaps, some discipline, some unique body of knowledge not found in any of the feeder disciplines, which performs the act of integration between these approaches—something more than a context only. If we simply say, 'Let us talk about our problems, using whatever ideas and supporting information that come to hand', then there will be no implicit claims being made. But once we give the activity a name—and indeed once we set up organizations under the name, once we establish a profession—we imply something with status, something which can be described as uniting the various areas of human activity to which linguistics can contribute: in short, we claim academic respectability and recognition. But, like the analogous discipline of education, applied linguistics has yet to demonstrate that it is anything other than an activity which draws people of similar interests together to discuss common problems as carefully as they can.

Now it may be, of course, that the careful discussion of common problems is all we can realistically demand, and that to ask for more is to misunderstand the nature of our various fields of interest. If this is so, however, it would be worth asking exactly what speech therapists or stylisticians find they can learn from the discussions of language teachers. It is perfectly possible—'education' is perhaps a case in point—for careful discussion of common problems to be conducted as rigorously as possible, without implying that all questions are capable of the same degree of formalization or rigour in their answering. Indeed, in educational circles a great deal of harm has been done by the enthusiasm of practitioners for inappropriate statistically-based experimental work, when discussion of a synthetic rather than analytic nature may have much greater value. There are academic dangers in formalism and practical risks in the adoption of inappropriate ritual. But it seems to me that applied linguistics is not in exactly the same position as education, that it is not simply an activity, but that it has within it the seeds of an integrated view of language applied to the world which should underly the work of all applied linguists. These seeds have not yet borne fruit; there are major areas of language activity—mother tongue teaching is perhaps the most notable—in which the major preoccupations of applied linguists have been seen as either irrelevant or dangerous. If applied linguistics is to be perceived as a fundamentally important discipline, this will only be when it produces ideas of sufficient generality to affect any language-using situation—when it performs the task of integrating all the various attitudes to language of researchers in other fields, and produces an account of language in use which is both convincing and readily comprehensible.

Where will such an account come from? There are, I think, some pointers. Over the last few years it has become increasingly apparent that there are intimate connections between psychological and sociological approaches to language. Studies of language acquisition have, as they have moved towards investigating the development of meaning, been forced to take a fuller account of situation (Halliday, 1975) and it is increasingly apparent that any account of the development of syntax (and even perhaps of phonology) cannot be isolated from the interaction of speaker and social environment. And this applies whether one is talking about language acquisition with mother tongue or second language. Furthermore, interesting similarities are being perceived between what used to be called language acquisition (mother tongue) and language learning (formally-based foreign or second language) (Corder, 1978), and these similarities do not only extend to the behaviour of the learners, or acquirers, themselves, but to the interactional behaviour of those who talk with them, whether teachers, parents, or people speaking to foreigners. More interesting still, these features of simplified language may be important in relation to the development, historically and geographically, of individual languages, in the relationships between languages, geographical dialects, pidgins, creoles and various kinds of functional dialect which have been discussed as registers of one sort or another (Schumann, 1978). What is beginning to emerge, in other words, is an account of language which is not static, idealized, and therefore not directly and simply applicable to the needs of workers of any kind with real problems. Rather it is an account which is dynamic, fluid, and increasingly motivated by reference to interaction, to active learning and using strategies associated with learners' responses to social demands. This is an account, in short, of users' application of language to the problems of the world and being in it. Such an integrated account is overdue, and in a number of spheres has been much in demand in reaction against too-simple transfers of the assumptions of traditional core linguistics to, for example, the classroom. The whole communicative movement in language teaching has been a reaction, in a variety of ways, to too narrow and 'syntactic' an interpretation of language teaching (Wilkins, 1972b, 1976; Widdowson, 1978, 1979). The so-called 'humanistic' approaches to language teaching, popular particularly in the States (Gattegno, 1976; Curran, 1976; Stevick, 1976), are attempts to increase the social and personal value of the language learning process. Such responses, coming from experienced teachers, have been received sympathetically on a wide front, but there is no systematic approach to language in society by which they can readily be explained or to which they can readily be referred. When such an account is fully developed (and it cannot be too far away) it will be an applied linguistic account, not a linguistic one, for at every point the emphasis will have to be on the interaction between language *use* (in relation to personal and group needs and the social environment) and language *development*, for the process of using and the process of developing (both of language by individuals and of langua*ges* by the uses they are put to by individuals) will be seen to be intimately related. Such an account cannot fail to have direct relevance to all those whose concern is the teaching of languages, the remediation of linguistic malfunction, the explanation of specific examples of linguistic performance, or any other application of linguistics.

An account such as I have outlined is, I suggest, a reasonable prediction. It is concerned, however, with a level of generality somewhat higher than the immediate concerns of many who call themselves applied linguists. Yet a detailed and systematic account of the nature of language development and change, linking individual motivated and unmotivated change with the historical development of languages, will provide a framework within which attempts to *cause* changes in linguistic behaviour can be described and evaluated. At the same time, such an account will allow activities such as teaching or speech therapy to be defined more positively in their relations to language use, for language will be seen as changing by its nature and by the uses to which it is put: the process of change will not be seen as deviant when the nature of change is more fully understood.

Mother Tongues, Second Languages and Foreign Languages: metaphors of goals against growth

(a slightly modified version of a paper presented at the Colloque de Berne, 1981)

The purpose of this paper is to examine many of the models and metaphors used in the discussion of language teaching, explicit or implicit, and to consider their value in relation to foreign, second and mother tongue teaching. The paper is partly motivated by a belief that all three types of teaching have been insufficiently sensitive to discussion concerned with the other areas, and have consequently been less efficient than they might have been in their practical activities. This is an issue which is particularly important for applied linguists, for their discipline has developed a tradition of concern for foreign language teaching, but has had comparatively little impact on, and consequently very little to say about, mother tongue teaching. If there is any genuine discipline seeking to apply linguistic insights, it must have a great deal of relevance to mother tongue work. If applied linguistics can find little to say of interest to mother tongue teachers, questions must be raised of its very status as a useful discipline.

I shall start by considering aspects of discussion in the mother tongue context in Britain. This discussion will be extended to embrace work with the mother tongue in other countries, and with mother tongues other than English. I shall then, but more briefly, consider comparable approaches to second and foreign language teaching, before relating the various approaches to each other in the final section.

Mother tongue teaching in Britain

The British educational scene of the last eighty years offers a curious combination, in English teaching, of unusual individual freedom coupled with a strong desire for some over-arching set of principles and aims to be imposed. There is a massive literature, from teachers, administrators, university professors, writers and literary critics, sociologists, politicians and philosophers, as well as linguists, about the desirable purposes of English teaching, appropriate procedures to use and defects of existing practices. The British school system is decentralized and held together mainly by the effects of formal examinations which tend to imitate each other and to influence the practice of teaching beyond the particular groups of students who are intended for any examination. In the past, employers and administrators, and the universities, have been the major influences on examining practice, but more recently teachers have become more influential and greater variety has been introduced. It is possible, however, to determine a number of approaches, though of course any one teacher or institution may combine any number of these to varying degrees. One classification of such approaches is as follows:

Aims

1. The promotion of skills:
   (a) Literacy and oracy
       (i) aiming at accuracy
       (ii) aiming at fluency and comfort;
   (b) Critical and analytical ability
       (i) specifically in response to writing or speech
       (ii) specifically in response to literary texts
       (iii) specifically in discussion of the nature of language and how it works
       (iv) by transfer, to all situations, particularly in response to aesthetic stimuli and to rational argument;
   (c) Social skills, 'poise', particularly in the context of the society of which the pupil is a member;
   (d) Use of the imagination.

2. Encouragement of attitudes and affective states:
   (a) Generally liberal, ethical, and humanitarian attitudes
       (i) through an active engagement with problems of writing and formulating ideas
       (ii) through response to works of literature;
   (b) Respect for the imagination and the intellect;
   (c) Respect for literary and cultural tradition
       (i) in general;
       (ii) a particular tradition.

3. Provision of information:
   (a) Knowledge about literature
       (i) the English literary tradition
       (ii) the Western literary tradition
       (iii) literature as a human activity;
   (b) Knowledge about language
       (i) the English language
       (ii) language as a human phenomenon.   (Brumfit, 1980: 15)

Different traditions in teaching have varied, of course in the emphases they have placed on different items in this taxonomy. In the 1970s particularly the promotion of skills has probably been seen as more important than provision of information, but at the same time there has been a strong movement to make teachers of English peculiarly responsible for the development of desirable social attitudes. Nonetheless, a typical pronouncement of the 1970s would be the following:

> A teacher of English starts from words and experiences, and a special interest in the dynamic relationship between them. He can look at this process from two points of view. First, it is concerned with producing language: both talking and writing; putting into words, and shaping and understanding by means of words, our reactions to experiences within and outside us. This we might call the *verbalization of experience*. Secondly, it is concerned with receiving language, both listening and reading; making sense of the words of others, and

understanding them in their context. This we might call the *experience of verbalization*, of what others have verbalized. It is thus concerned with improving a pupil's competence in using his mother tongue.

(Stratta, Dixon and Wilkinson, 1973: xi)

It should be noted that these intentions run counter to some contemporary linguistic doctrine, at least at first sight, insofar as they refer to oracy as well as literacy. There have indeed been spokesmen for the view that schools should rightly be concerned only with literacy, and their position is certainly persuasive. But the notion of differential competence in speech as well as in writing is widely—probably universally—accepted by English teachers. At the same time, however, there has also been concern that oracy should be developed, not simply because it is desirable for citizens to be articulate in speech, but because— according to one influential school of thought—the process of mastering speech and developing oral capacities is a necessary prerequisite for successful literacy (Britton, 1970; Barnes, Britton and Rosen, 1969).

Any demand for the natural development of speech or writing forces us to focus on the contexts in which language will be produced, and discussion of such contexts leads to a consideration of the second and third elements in our taxonomy. Many writers, particularly those who approach English teaching with a concern for moral values associated with response to literature and deriving from the work of the literacy critic F. R. Leavis (see, for example, Leavis, 1933; Leavis and Thompson, 1933), are particularly concerned with the quality of the environment, threatened by the values of industrial society. This concern may be combined with a concern for the development of the imagination. A representative position is that of David Holbrook:

Our minimum aim is to develop powers of imagination in every child so that the school leaver has had some experience, in phantasy, of the major adult problems of living (he is, of course, already beginning to face them in his life). Every child should gather thereby that such problems are common to all mankind, and are not with varying degrees of moral quality. Even the weakest pupil should have at one time or another felt deeply about a story or a poem, so that the experience provides a sense of balance, the enlargement of sympathy, and a grasp of values.

(Holbrook, 1961: 27)

It is not in fact a major leap from here to a position which may appear to emphasize the process to the total exclusion of the product:

What should children be asked to write about? Anything, providing it can stimulate their imaginations, move their feelings, arouse their curiosities.

(Abbs, 1969: 66)

But this position is more likely to be geared towards a larger ambition. English may be seen as attempting to break down the isolation of the individual (Flowers, 1966), as serving the inward needs of children, providing therapy through imaginative work (Holbrook, 1964), or as assisting socialization (Bullock, 1975).

At the same time, the older issues of the literary tradition continued to be pressed:

> The English teacher's province . . . includes the transmission of a great literature, together with some sense of the wider culture from which that literature sprang; the custody of a great language.
>
> (Hollindale, 1972: 335)

Indeed this concern, being somewhat unfashionable, especially when it concentrates on simple acquisition of knowledge, is probably voiced less often than it is felt. A student of mine remarked in 1974 that 'an English child needs to know about Shakespeare and Dickens and Wordsworth, and what they wrote, just as he needs to know about the Bible, the Spanish Armada, and Winston Churchill'. The general acceptance of this remark by the rest of the seminar group reflects, I suspect, a wider agreement. Nor need we be necessarily worried by such a view. As long as the accumulation of knowledge is seen as the acquisition of tokens which build up a systematic picture of the culture within which students are learning to operate—in which the language, historical tradition and literature are all cultural tokens—it will perform a valuable function in assisting self-definition. Only when such learning is meaningless because it is unstructured is it useless.

Such a concern with knowledge need not be limited to literary knowledge, however. Several British linguists, including Quirk, Halliday, Sinclair and Crystal have concerned themselves with the role of linguistics in the classroom. In 1967, in a collection aimed at English teachers, Halliday was insisting that

> Children can learn about language, and be fascinated by the process. They can become fully involved in the study of its grammar, even in the primary school, especially if linguistics can provide a "concrete semantics" for operations with language leading to the development of basic general concepts, on the analogy of the physical operations used to develop concepts of weight, volume and the like. Is there any place for this approach?
>
> (Halliday, 1967: 88-89)

But faced with such diversity of intention, it is difficult to know how to react. One clear danger, which was raised at the seminal Dartmouth conference (when British and American teachers of English met to discuss general issues of the teaching of English as a mother tongue), is that 'anything that anyone thinks is good for youngsters can be dumped into the course because it involves some use of language' (cited in Canham, 1972: 59). Indeed, it is sometimes hard to take such determination to suck everything into English teaching very seriously. When the British Association for Applied Linguistics in 1973 drafted its submission to the Bullock Committee it commented that 'such large purposes are proper to a whole educational system rather than to one part (even though an important part) of it'. But there is no doubt that the conflicts and contradictions found in the discussion of English teaching in Britain and the States can be found elsewhere as well. Dixon (1967, 1975), in what is the clearest statement of informed contemporary opinion on English teaching in Britain, refers to the current model as a growth model, in contrast with the skills model found largely in junior schools and the heritage model found in secondary schools. To some extent a growth model reflects a synthesis of many of the elements isolated in our earlier taxonomy, whereas the skills model fitted most closely with section 1, and the heritage model with sections 2 and 3. But the analogy is not exact, for a growth model must, if it is to be at all principled, provide some stated goals, and it is difficult to see how these can be defined except in terms of the other two models. It makes very little sense to claim that 'growth' is in itself virtuous, unless we all aspire to the condition of the (extinct, but undoubtedly well-grown) dinosaur! But it makes very good sense, as we shall see when we consider foreign language teaching, to relate the concept of growth to a methodology for achieving explicitly stated goals.

Mother tongue teaching outside Britain

In 1972 the Council for Cultural Co-operation of the Council of Europe published a report (Marshall, 1972) on mother tongue teaching in the final years of academic secondary schools in member states. The conclusions shed interesting light on the themes of our discussion so far. The study of literature in the mother tongue, particularly, seems to have taken over the humanizing role which was formerly the prerogative of classical studies. This would appear to correspond to the heritage model, but the study of literature also has 'functional' (skill) and 'personality development' (growth) elements as well (p.63). Language work is rarely done formally, but the role of linguistics is discussed.

> It is possible, however, that the findings of linguistics may help to give a more structured approach to the teaching of language, and it is felt that an element of linguistics should be included in the professional education of the intending teacher of the mother tongue. It seems that linguistics are already modifying the teaching of language and that a far more liberal approach is gradually being adopted, giving greater importance to the pupil's own language. The concept of 'appropriate' language now tends to replace that of 'correct' language.
>
> (Marshall, 1972: 63)

Descriptive work on language is seen to be increasing (in contrast with Britain), but literature is still the predominant study, with relatively little access to foreign literature in translation. Literary history is less important than it was, so there is a tendency for texts to be discussed in relative isolation. Most exercises are written rather than oral, but a shift is noted towards 'a more liberal attitude towards the study of language and of literature' and it is suggested that 'the role of the mother tongue will be seen first and foremost to be the development of an instrument of communication' (p.63). Once again, we may observe a certain confusion as literature, linguistics and personal growth jostle for position within a limited timetable.

In the same year that the Council of Europe report was published another report appeared from the UNESCO Institute of Education in Hamburg. This (Canham, 1972) reported a seminar on mother tongue teaching with participants from USA, Britain, Argentina, Jordan, Switzerland, Ethiopia, the Soviet Union and France. The discussion had followed a similar pattern, with the same kind of preoccupations, as those we have already noted. The only additional point worth making is that the delegates from outside Europe were perhaps more concerned with the notion of correctness than the Europeans and Americans. But generally the impression remains of considerable uncertainty: the old order has certainly changed, but not yet yielded place to a new.

I have been unable to obtain more recent information about mother tongue teaching in the major European countries, but it is worth making one comment on an observable tendency in Britain which, I suspect, is paralleled in a number of other countries. This is the beginning of a questioning of the whole concept of 'mother tongue'. To some extent this questioning may have developed from the 'more liberal attitude' referred to by Marshall. It is also in part a response (in Britain at least) to the presence of a large number of mother tongues in the country which are not English. These did indeed exist before, but recent immigration patterns have led to increasing recognition of their existence, together with an increasing sensitivity to the role of indigenous non-English mother tongues (James, 1978), and to linguistic diversity within English itself (Rosen and Burgess, 1980). The effect of this has been to lead to questioning of the concept of the mother tongue. It is too early to say what effect such questioning will have on the practice of language teaching, but it is an important trend which will be commented on later in this paper.

Second and foreign language teaching

'Second language teaching' is an ambiguous term. Within the British tradition it refers to two distinct phenomena. It was originally used to distinguish English teaching in countries where English had a social role to play, as in many ex-colonial countries, from teaching English as a foreign language in countries where it had no role to play for internal use (see Bright and McGregor, 1970). More recently the teaching of English to non-native speakers in Britain, when those speakers are intending to settle, has taken over the term. Although this language teaching situation is clearly second language by the earlier definition, it also involves many political and social considerations which separate it from overseas second language teaching. Second language teaching in Britain is interesting for our argument in that it is the only language teaching tradition which has developed independently of the classical tradition. Both foreign language teaching and second language teaching overseas have had, albeit in somewhat diluted form, the same kind of confusions and difficulties which we have already noted in the discussion of mother tongue teaching. They too have experienced skills and heritage models, and are being tempted by growth models at the moment. Second language teaching in Britain, having arrived later as an organized force, started with a heavy skills orientation and has moved to a heavy growth model with strong socio-political overtones. Unfortunately there has been comparatively little reporting or investigation of what actually happens in language teaching classes of this type, and sophisticated theoretical discussion has been minimal. But it does offer us a convenient contrast to much other foreign language teaching.

Second language teaching in Britain started by taking over a strong foreign language teaching skills-orientated model (Derrick, 1966), but has shifted gradually but relatively inexplicitly towards a growth model, mainly in reaction to the manifest deficiencies of the harder forms of skills model. The most extreme position has been reached by the current BBC television series, 'Speak for Yourself', in which the language used is relatively unsimplified, and the situations of major social and political relevance. The reaction of second language teachers to this have been extremely mixed, as correspondence in local Second Language Teachers' newsletters attests, but the programmes do reflect a widely held expert view which diminishes the explicit language component and increases the social content. (There is still extended, functionally based, language back-up available— Gubbay and Cogill, 1980—but the overall conception reflects the ideas of Freire, 1971, as well as, more distantly, functional-notional approaches as in van Ek, 1975, and Wilkins, 1976.)

'Speak for Yourself' was aimed largely at adult audiences, but similar movements have been at work in schools through local authority teachers' centres of various kinds. It is probably fair to say that such centres have been moving towards a functional basis—empirically—ahead of the more theoretical discussion in foreign language teaching circles. At the same time, though, the basis of language teaching concerns has been steadily broadening. 'Teaching English to Immigrants' has turned into 'Multi-racial Education' and, more recently, into 'Multi-cultural Education'. This move has been largely beneficial, but it does carry the risk that language issues may disappear, or be seen as merely technical and trivial. Language work is, however, being increasingly related to the mother tongue issue, for there is a strong movement to co-ordinate the teaching of English with the maintenance of the mother tongue. Again, the movement is motivated more by political considerations than linguistic ones at the moment, but this intersection between linguistic and community issues is potentially of great interest, and connects with the definition problems referred to earlier.

Foreign language teaching theory scarcely needs documenting here, for many of the most important recent developments have been outlined in previous colloquia (Neuchâtel and Berne) and can be found in the proceedings, or in collections which draw heavily on these and the work of the Council of Europe, such as Brumfit and Johnson, 1979. There has been an increasing move towards a more functional approach (Widdowson, 1978), but the impetus towards anything like a growth model has come from quite other sources than applied linguistics. Stevick (1976) has outlined his own dissatisfaction with traditional approaches and indicated how a concern to relate language learning to the deeper impulses of students led him to an interest in fringe methodologies: Counselling learning, developed by the psychiatrist Charles Curran (1976), the Silent Way, developed by Caleb Gattegno (1976), and Suggestopaedia, developed by the Bulgarian psychologist Georgi Lozanov. Only the first of these can be closely related to the growth model, but all the methods, in very different ways, attempt to increase motivation by lowering the cognitive threshold of students. Stevick's book, however, and the discussion which it provoked, together with the direct impact of these methodologies, led to a greater and greater interest in creative approaches to language learning, and many materials now appearing on the market reflect this influence. In the final section I shall try to relate these trends to others within the other language teaching fields.

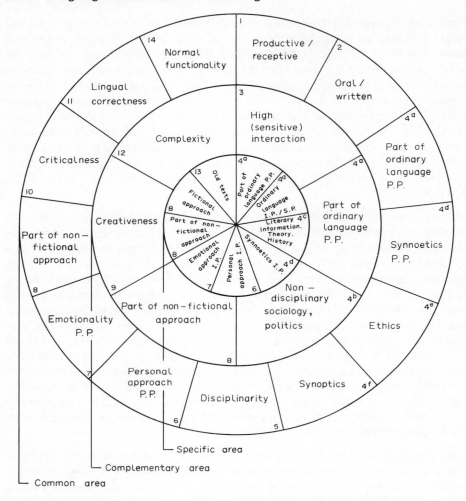

Relationships between languages and language teaching

Probably the most ambitious recent attempt to construct a theory of mother tongue teaching is ten Brinke's 'The Complete Mother-Tongue Curriculum' (ten Brinke, 1976). While the apparatus is somewhat cumbersome, there are parts which are worth noting, particularly the attempt to define the areas of mother tongue teaching which are specific to the subject (on the basis of observed practice) and those which are complementary. These areas represent the *de facto* maximum and minimum size of specific mother tongue concern. Other concerns, which he refers to as the common area in the diagram (ten Brinke, 1976: 231), are as much the concerns of other subject specializations. The areas of unique concern to mother tongue teaching are (a) the concern with old texts in the mother tongue, (b) some concerns with ordinary language for practical purposes, (c) ordinary language used for intellectual purposes, and for traditional purposes, (d) literary information, theory and history, (e) talking about oneself, (f) talking personally about a subject, (g) emotional approaches for intellectual purposes, (h) fiction, and (i) some parts of non-fiction.

For our present purposes it is unnecessary to elaborate the model in detail, though there would be some value in applying it with care to second and foreign teaching situations. It is worth observing, though that all of these values have some function in the foreign language classroom, though the motivation for including them will differ from that of the mother tongue situation. However, there will be no *necessary* demand for these in the foreign language, for—unlike with the mother tongue—a foreign language is always something of a luxury. What is clear, though, is that there are three factors in mother tongue teaching which have revealed themselves in all the discussion we have investigated, and that all of these have some relationship to foreign language teaching. These are the concern with personal expression, which needs to be adapted to the needs of society, so that the growth and skills models can be seen as complementary aspects of the same phenomenon—corresponding approximately to Halliday's mathetic and pragmatic categories, for a total separation of the two functions seems to oppose contemporary interpretations of language development. And a concern with literature and tradition, which can in principle be separated from the other concerns.

At this point it is worth pointing out a convenient parallel with one branch of contemporary discussion of foreign language teaching, for all language teaching seems to have a tendency to move towards content, whether literary, descriptive linguistic, cultural or political. One line of approach in foreign language teaching is to see this tendency as a recognition that a truly functional approach to language teaching must give us a content to function with, and a truly notional approach must give us a basis for conceptual development. Consequently, the arguments for teaching language through a subject area in the second language setting (Widdowson, 1968) or through literature or culture in a foreign language setting (Widdowson and Brumfit, 1981) remain compelling in terms of current communicative models. The problem is that the issue has rarely been addressed very seriously. ESP has tended to concentrate overmuch on the language issue, and traditional subject teaching has tended to take language too much for granted. The problem is by no means simple, for it depends on a far fuller understanding of the relationship between problem-solving, socialization and language development than we so far have available. The skills model neglects the crucial issues of function and content, the growth model neglects the issue of objectives, while the heritage model performs a distinct and valuable function which risks neglecting language development altogether. The answer must be, not to reject any of these models completely, but to endeavour to understand the relationships between them more completely, in order to make explicit the value of traditional practice.

But to understand these relationships will be dependent on a more theoretical development, which has already been referred to. The more closely we examine mother tongue situations, the less clear is it what we mean by the term 'mother tongue'. Not only do we have problems in establishing the boundaries between dialects and languages in multilingual settings, especially if the languages are closely related to each other, but in multilingual settings there are also difficulties in distinguishing between the first-learnt language, the language of the home, the most frequently used language, and the language of basic cognitive and/or emotional development. The 'mother tongue' of school use is rarely the same dialect as that used at home, and often not the same language. In many countries, for good economic and political reasons, it is not possible for the language of school to be that of early development, yet clearly there are some languages which are closer to being 'mother-tongue-like' than others. Now that we are more conscious of the implications of multilingualism in schools, we stand a greater chance of understanding the complex relationships between personal growth, the compromises necessary to achieve communication with our fellows, and the various cognitive demands made on us by subject matter of different kinds. These relationships are not only central to language teaching, but to all education, and indeed to all human activity, since language is such a central element in human relationships. It seems likely that just as the presence of many non-native speakers of standard European languages has led us to question our attitudes to dialect speakers who have always been in our schools in large numbers, so the serious exploration of educational development in multilingual contexts will lead us to understand more fully the whole process of education. The problems of 'foreign', 'second' and 'mother tongue' teaching can no longer be seen as independent.

Out of this discussion a number of areas for investigation emerge. One is the historical dimension. The concept of 'mother tongue' was particularly important in the emerging educational systems of the nineteenth century, and discussion of the ways in which language decisions were made, both in European countries and in the colonies, will provide an important perspective. The 'mother tongue' may be perceived as an instrument of centralization, even of repression, as a result of such studies. (See, for example, Bamgbose, 1976; Brumfit, Ann, 1980). Other areas include more precise attempts to delineate the relationships between dialect variation within one language community, leading to examinations of the personal functions, for users, of language variation; the pedagogical implications of a growth model across languages in multilingual situations; and theoretical issues in the psychology of bilingual situations. The last area links with important issues raised by Professor Sinclair in a paper for this colloquium: to what extent is it possible for learners to develop abilities beyond what they attain in their mother tongues, and what are the conditions to assist them to do so, if any? Questions of this kind are going to become more and more important in language teaching.

Yet, however much we emphasize the divisive effects of linguistic domination, in a world of increasing contact there is no way in which it can be completely avoided. The process of growing up and being educated in the contemporary world is unavoidably one of linguistic extension. The model below, with which this paper concludes, is an attempt to depict the expansion of linguistic capacity which will necessarily be associated with socialization and education. Somewhat schematically, the terminology of linguists, and educationalists, has been related to the development of the individual's linguistic environment throughout the period of preparation for life.

Linguists descriptive categories		Major conventional choices	Educational tendencies in language
Language(s)	International contact	Range as capable	L_1/L_2 or FL
Standard language + varied dialects	Wider world	Range as required	L_1 or L_2
Standard language	Education	Literacy/social dialects (as administratively allowed)	L_1 or L_2
Dialect(s)	Social environment	Social dialects (varying in range)	L_1/L_2
Dialect	Family	Baby-talk → in-group talk → limited social dialects	L_1/MT
Idiolect	Mother	Baby-talk	L_1/MT

Time ↑

Individual sociolingual development
(communicative competence)

Cross section:

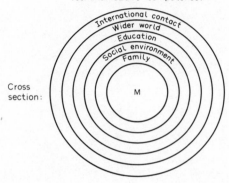

International contact
Wider world
Education
Social environment
Family
M

Section Three:

CRITICISMS OF CURRENT PRACTICE

The eight papers in this section are diverse in level and type, but they are all part of a critical commentary on current argument and practice. The first three are—I hope—my final statements on the syllabus design and methodology discussions which have preoccupied so many language teaching theorists in the past decade. The next three are—again I hope final—statements on the humanistic movement. These doubts have been discussed by various people, and by no means convince everybody, but the 'Humanistic doubts . . .' paper does represent my own position most fully, and does attempt to relate my approach to the theory and practice of language teaching to a broader and deeper concern with our role as thinking and feeling human beings. The seventh paper addresses the issue of grading, which is currently rather neglected in theoretical discussion. And the final paper, by way of light relief, swipes in as many directions as possible in as short a time as possible. I hope sometime to develop the copyright issue (number 7 of the final paper) into a more careful argument, but I have not yet been able to find the time to do so as thoroughly as would be necessary to convince the doubting publishers and authors, who seem to be almost unanimously against my position.

From Defining to Designing:
communicative specifications versus communicative methodology in foreign language teaching

(a paper presented at the ACTFL/Goethe Institut Conference, New York, October 1979, and published in *Studies in Second Language Acquisition*, Indiana University Press, 1980)

Introductory note

The following paper is an attempt to explore some of the implications of viewing language learning as a process which is not based on a view of a static product. Language use, we can increasingly see, is not the use of a set of definable and prearranged tokens, but is a process of linguistic and cultural negotiation of meaning. Students have to develop their innate ability to use language for their own purposes in interaction with the purposes of other language users. Communicative syllabuses have been discussed partly through a recognition of this need, but a discussion of syllabus organization is not enough, for the methodological implications are much more important. If languages are not, in principle, discrete, language teaching will not be served well if it is based on the assumption that we can specify the learner's product exactly. All syllabuses tend to concentrate on the product, or content. This paper argues that it is time to move away from syllabus definition, which has now been adequately discussed for the current state of classroom practice.

The literature on communicative course design is extensive (see Shaw, 1977, for an overview) and it would not be an unfair generalization to say that, in Britain at least, applied linguistics has related to language teaching most powerfully through discussions of course design. But, perhaps inevitably, there has also been a feeling in the language teaching profession that theory has outrun practice, so that the last few years have been a period of consolidation rather than advance, as new ideas have been tested, adapted and revised in the light of experience. Time and place have adhered neatly, for just as a wealth of insight has been available from the work of social psychologists, sociolinguists, social anthropologists and philosophers a massive demand has developed for courses in English for overseas learners while the British economy has been desperately in need of foreign exchange and relatively accessible to at least the richer overseas countries. It is scarcely surprising, then, that courses have been developed which claim to exploit such insights in the service of the overseas client. Yet the urgency and intensity of the demands of the insatiable market pose a threat as well as a challenge, and there is a serious risk of genuine innovation being buried under a mass of marketing material as acronyms tumble over each other to reach, with unscientific haste, the next government, multinational corporation, or united nations body willing to have its pocket picked.

One problem is that the serious evaluation and integration of insights gained from such a broad selection of disciplines demands an unusually broad-ranging and acute mind. However, such interdisciplinary difficulties are central to any applied discipline. More worrying in practice has been the problem of relating what are essentially descriptive procedures to the needs of language classrooms. Learning is not describing, and if we are truly to utilize insights from various sciences, we must learn to convert description to process. Careful discussion of how to do this in language teaching has scarcely begun. Indeed, it is rarely seen as a problem. Wilkins (1972, 1976) attacks traditional grammatical syllabuses for a number of defects, but proposes to substitute as a basis a series of categories which describe interaction rather than grammar. Such categories are open to the same objections which he raises against grammatical syllabuses (see Brumfit, 1980a, pp. 98-106, for an elaboration of this argument). What has happened is that syllabuses are increasingly being specified in terms of interactional behaviour expectations, which often is extremely useful pragmatically. When strong theoretical claims are not made, discussion may be helpful (e.g. Jupp and Hodlin, 1975), but it can be misleading to imply that fundamental general principles are being developed (Munby, 1978). There is no question that behavioural specifications have a value in *testing*—that is, they indicate a relationship between the syllabus and the real world, they tell us when we can stop teaching—but it is by no means clear that they have any direct relation to our *teaching* procedures, for a number of reasons.

The major reason is that a system for the production of utterances cannot be identified with the output of the system. What we are teaching is a generative system which all human beings have a capacity to acquire. We are not teaching a limited set of behaviours, but a capacity to produce those behaviours—a capacity which cannot help enabling its user to do many other behaviours than those specified by any limited set. Furthermore, since the system which we are teaching has close relations to the most intimate thoughts and feelings of the learner, it poses a challenge, if not an assault on the learner's view of the world. This is because we use language, as has been widely observed, simultaneously to interact with others—pragmatically—and to make sense of the world to ourselves—mathetically, to use Halliday's term (Halliday, 1975, 1979). We operate simultaneously on the social and the internal levels, and the two cannot be totally separated from each other, with important implications for pedagogy which have been widely discussed in recent years from a variety of different points of view (e.g. Stevick, 1976; Curran, 1976; Gattegno, 1976; Maley and Duff, 1978; Brumfit, 1978).

To use slightly archaic terminology, then, we can reject a list of behavioural specifications as the prime input to a syllabus on the grounds that it is a specification of items of sociolinguistic performance which cannot be identified with sociolinguistic competence. But the issue is more complex than such a formulation would suggest, because the learner/user of language does not have a passive relationship with such competence. We do not acquire a set of rules which we have to accept; rather we acquire a set of strategies for interaction which we manipulate for our various purposes, constantly negotiating and renegotiating our linguistic relationships. With language, as with any other semiotic system, we construct and we play, adapt and refine, stretch and twist and break the components of the system in order to create new messages, for ourselves or for others. We acquire a flexible, dynamic system, and the process of acquisition must itself be flexible and dynamic.

Now any discussion of syllabus design must recognize the features of language which have been referred to above, but the syllabus must recognize other constraints also. A syllabus is a way of describing something which must be learnt for pedagogic purposes, and the chief characteristic of an educational institution is its focusing function; that is an educational institution acts as a physical and temporal focus for learning. The limitations in time and place provide the major differences between formal and informal learning: there is an implicit promise in the act of setting up an educational institution that the procedures used will in some sense be more efficient than the more or less random procedures of informal learning in the world outside. And a syllabus is a statement of efficient learning; indeed it can be seen as a metaphor for the human learning process. When we organize a syllabus in a school, we are attempting to organize our material in the way which reflects most closely the processes of learning in the human mind, in order to facilitate the process. We are saying, in effect, that to approach the material to be learnt in this way is more efficient than to approach it in other available ways. Only if we view the learning process as totally random can we avoid the responsibility of attempting to organize our syllabuses in a way which best reflects our understanding of human learning. In other words, syllabus design must be responsive to learning theory.

There is a further important point to be made, which is that everything we know about human learning suggests that it is crucially dependent on our ability, consciously or subconsciously, to systematize. All other things being equal, learning will be effective when the material being presented is capable of being interpreted systematically. Furthermore, a system is more than a list, for it cannot avoid being theoretically based in that the relations between the parts need to be describable in terms which are capable of some degree of generalization; indeed the relations between the parts will probably be more important than the specific parts themselves, for it is on the basis of these relations that the learner will perceive the system.

All this may appear rather too abstract, but it has a direct bearing on language learning, for language can be presented both systematically and unsystematically, and much of the recent discussion on syllabus design has been concerned with the relative merits of rival systems of linguistic description. Perhaps it is worth making the argument specific by reference to lists of functions. There have been a number of attempts to specify the needs of learners in terms of linguistic functions (van Ek, 1975; Wilkins, 1976; Munby, 1978), but all of them suffer from the defect of having produced a list rather than a system. Until it is possible to produce a finite list of functions, and to show the relations between each separate one, it will not be possible to discuss them theoretically at all, for each scholar can pluck new examples out of the air whenever the need arises. This is not to say, of course, that such lists do not have a useful role to play in syllabus design, but simply that they cannot be discussed seriously as the major *basis* for a syllabus with pretensions to be systematic.

It is worth perhaps adding at this point that the situation is further confused by the difficulty of evaluating comparatively various kinds of syllabus organization or methodologies. There are so many variables to control that there is no possibility of producing a serious experiment without distorting the complexity of the teaching situation to such an extent that it loses all contact with reality. Furthermore, learners *will* learn some language from any sort of exposure to it, so that it is difficult, if not impossible, to demonstrate beyond any shadow of doubt the superiority of one particular approach over another. This is mainly because teaching is the expression of a relationship between teacher and taught, and will—indeed must—vary whenever one of the parties changes. At the same time, however, it is still possible to behave in the classroom in a more or less principled manner, and the principles can be discussed as carefully as possible. It may not be unfair to claim, though, that these principles are to assist *teachers* to think as clearly as they can, rather than directly to describe the process, objectively perceived, that the student goes through. Most students, after all, only go through a particular stage of the learning process once, but the teacher has to repeat the same stage several times over. It may be fair to say that students will learn, providing that they are presented with systematically organized language, but that teachers need to modify the systems they use if they are not to lose all enthusiasm through constant repetition of procedures!

We may agree, then, that a syllabus is necessary and that it should be based on a systematic view of the nature of language. However, a syllabus must also be capable of being broken down into discrete elements, for education takes place in real time, and is, in practice, segmented. The traditional concerns with selection, grading and sequencing (Mackey, 1965) remain as important now as ever. But it is at this point that the desire to be fully systematic must be thwarted. It is certainly possible to adopt as a basis for a syllabus any well worked out descriptive system, but implementation is never tidy. A syllabus cannot but involve generalization, but it must be generalization from local conditions, and local conditions impose their own constraints. Thus any practical syllabus will have to take into account such factors as the mother tongue(s) of the students, the nature of the language teaching tradition (for example, does it create particular expectations in primary school about the nature of language learning, indeed does the primary school methodology make specific types of error likely to occur?), the administrative support available, and the intensity and quantity of language instruction. Such features will be part of the specification of a realistic syllabus, but they are not capable of being incorporated into a true system, as defined above, for of course many of these features are not features of language itself. Indeed, if a practical syllabus should express the relationship between teachers, students and the conditions in which they work (including but not limited to the materials), then we need to know a great deal more than we do not only about different groups of learners, but also about different groups of teachers. At the same time, it should be possible to outline fairly clearly what needs to be done, even if we are not in a position to do it at once.

Let me first outline a realistic procedure for syllabus design in a normal educational system, before considering the radical critique of even the most communicative conventional syllabus. A realistic syllabus must start with a relationship between what is needed and learning theory. Clearly, since a syllabus is necessarily a generalization to accommodate a number of different students, both the needs and the learning processes implicit will be generalized, but the needs specification should be able to incorporate reasonably appropriate predictions of the purposes for which students will need the target language, and—more trivially—of the settings in which they may be expected to operate. Such specifications will clarify immediately whether the language necessary is genuine language or whether language-like behaviour will suffice. (It is necessary to make this point because there has been a great deal of confusion in the discussion of teaching language for specific purposes. Some 'specific purpose' courses are simply rescue operations to enable students to produce appropriate responses in an extremely limited code, which may incidentally use the lexis and a simplified grammar of a particular language (airline pilots), or which involves a highly predictable selection, heavily determined by context, from the target language (waiters). Valuable as such teaching may be, it does not provide us with a satisfactory model for other types of purpose-directed language teaching, for its aim, in the first instance at least, is not language behaviour, but language-like behaviour—though of course the human language-learning capacity is such that even on the basis of such courses students *may* continue to develop genuine generative systems which transcend the limitations of the course. The genuine language learning courses—similar to, but not overlapping completely with those distinguished as English for Academic Purposes rather than English for Occupational Purposes—will require learners to operate a native-speaker-like generative system. The fundamental question raised is whether such a system will be different in any fundamental way between groups of widely varying needs: how different do the *systems* for literary critics, physicists, lawyers, soldiers or diplomats need to be? This, of course, is a quite different point from the one that motivation may be improved by a concentration on material of direct vocational interest—though there is a great deal of anecdotal evidence emerging to question even this.)

Let me return, then to the original argument. If, as is most often the case, genuine language is required, the specification of needs has provided us with a situational context for the teaching, but—for reasons outlined earlier in this paper—it has not provided us with a system which can be related at all to learning theory, however conceived. And, in the present state of our knowledge, it is difficult to see how any system other than the grammatical system can be related in this way to learning. Allowing for fuzziness at the edges, the grammatical system gives us a generative framework which is, by being generative, economical and capable of being systematically ordered for teaching (teaching, as distinct from learning, being necessarily linear). That is, it is possible to segment the grammatical system, and to order the segments according to some view of the relations between the parts. It is possible to move from the simple to the complex, using internal criteria of complexity (in, for example, the verb group) if we believe that moving from simple to complex imitates most effectively the nature of human language learning. If we hold some other belief, we can similarly relate it to the relations between the items in the grammatical system. There is, to repeat, no way in which a similar process can be followed with an inventory of functions, or even a list of notional categories, as used either by Wilkins (1976) or van Ek (1975).

There is a pragmatic reason, also, for not rejecting the grammatical basis for syllabus design. Apart from the instinctive feeling that it is arrogant to assume that generations of language teachers and linguists were all wrong quite so fundamentally, there is also the inevitable necessity of building our syllabuses on the experience of the past. In practice, a syllabus is partly an anticipation of learner difficulties, and such difficulties have been discussed in the past very much in grammatical terms. We know a great deal about the problems of particular groups of learners, and we can help such learners acquire the syntax of the target language without making some of the mistakes made by our predecessors. A refusal to utilize the kind of knowledge expressed in, for example, Alexander *et al.* (1975), implies an irresponsibly dogmatic break with the past. Of course, the generalized syllabus outlined has to be modified to particular circumstances, even in relation to syntax, but in most parts of the world there is a wealth of similar experience to draw upon.

However, the kind of grammatical syllabus outlined above can be no more than a starting point, even on its own terms. Each generalization must be modified to particular circumstances, and the process of modification is a pragmatic one, not a theoretical one. That is, it is crucially dependent on the experience of teachers working with similar classes and similar conditions to those for which the syllabus is being designed. Once again, having accepted the need for a systematic *basis*, we have to become unsystematic in part at least of our implementation. How do we make sense out of this lack of system?

The simplest proposal is to use the grammatical system as the core of the syllabus in a series of stages, like a ladder, but to be prepared to relate all other material essential to the syllabus to the series of stages. Thus notional, functional and situational specifications can be conceived of as a spiral round a basically grammatical core (Brumfit, 1981).

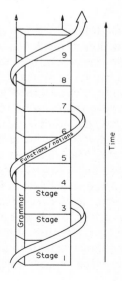

Such a design has the advantage that functions and notions are not treated as if they can be taught discretely; they can be related appropriately to grammatical exponents, and a process of *bargaining* can be introduced at each stage between the elements in the spiral and those in the core. And, indeed, this is a process which is visible in many traditional second and foreign language course books. First units frequently dealt with *greetings* or *introductions*—that is, they were primarily functional; later units frequently included items like *purpose, concession* or *result*—that is, they were primarily notional. But the introduction of such categories did not prevent the basic progression through the economical, generative grammatical system.

But a design such as this is not yet complete, even before we consider methodology, for every serious syllabus for practical purposes should incorporate a range of items which will not fit neatly into the system. These may be observed errors which will require remedial treatment with some students but not with others, areas of linguistic knowledge (for example, work on syllable recognition) which experience has shown to facilitate acquisition of aspects of the linguistic system, or simply information about the target culture which is appropriate at a particular stage in the course. Such items need to be slotted in to the system, but the appropriate place to do this may be determined by external factors, or by the needs of a particular class. A practical syllabus must, therefore, include a checklist of material which may be either compulsory or optional. If compulsory, the decision about where to slot in to the system will be the teacher's; if optional, the decision about whether and where to slot in will rest with the teacher; in either case no syllabus which is realistic can afford to neglect such checklists. The process of practical syllabus design can thus be seen to be one of starting with a genuine descriptive system, and modifying it in relation to external constraints to a system imposed by the demands of real time. Sometimes the matching of these two systems will be arbitrary; this is unavoidable, but it will not be random.

The procedure which has been outlined above may appear to be a return to everything that was bad about traditional grammatical syllabuses, with merely a few cosmetic modifications. It does not directly confront the implied criticisms of writers who take a more methodological position than Wilkins, Widdowson (e.g. 1978), Munby or van Ek. Newmark (1966) and Allwright (1977), for example, have suggested that it is not the nature of syllabuses which are wrong, but the concept of syllabuses. Both, in very different ways, have called for less interference by teachers in the language learning process. It is not difficult to demonstrate that teacher responsibility includes having some systematic way of determining when to appear and when to disappear, and I do not propose to repeat this argument now (see Brumfit, 1977), but the radical critique can be usefully related to the earlier argument to isolate an interesting shift of emphasis. Many of the features of the communicative syllabuses were previously thought of as matters of methodology rather than of syllabus description. That is, they related to the process of contextualization which the teacher was expected to perform through classroom activity. Such methodological activity was often ineffective, and proponents of communicative syllabuses looked to recent developments in linguistic and sociological theory to restore an appropriate perspective, and—by implication—to improve teaching methodology. But both the old and the new syllabus designers concentrate on the code, on what is to be taught and what it is to be taught for. The process of acquisition has been less fully discussed, though attempts are now being made to generalize from our understanding of language in movement to teaching in classrooms (Corder, 1979), and the work of Schumann (1978) and others is likely to be very influential. What makes critics such as Allwright interesting, however, is the recognition of the intimate relation between language acquisition and language use, and the attempt to simulate language use as fully as possible. There has been a great deal of discussion of formal and informal learning environments recently, but—from the point of view of conventional school situations where most language teaching takes place—little of it has offered direct and helpful support. What we need is a return to the serious discussion of methodology, not in the sense of useful teaching tips, of which there are plenty available, but in the sense of careful discussion of the role and behaviour of teachers and students related to the demands of communicative syllabuses, because communicative syllabuses have not helped us to convert the static descriptive systems of linguists, social psychologists or philosophers into learning activity, dynamic use of a dynamic system. Indeed, the discussion of communicative syllabuses has caused us to concentrate far too much on what we teach and what we teach for, so that we have lost sight of the fact that effective learning depends on a vast amount of language work which is *not* responding to new items in the syllabus. Essentially, syllabuses are concerned with *accuracy* (even the concern for appropriacy must have a normative element in the foreign language situation), but students have to learn to be *fluent* as well as accurate, and at the early stages the conditions for achieving one are incompatible with the conditions for achieving the other. We need, therefore, classroom activities for accuracy, and these will relate to new input as specified by the syllabus, and we need classroom activities for fluency, and these will relate to the most effective language use possible *with the system which the student currently operates*. It is true that at the advanced stages of learning some elements of both may be combined, but in the early stages a demand for formally evaluated accuracy inevitably inhibits fluency. The justification for raising fluency work to a level comparable with traditional accuracy work is that through fluency work each student has the opportunity to operate individual strategies, because the teacher is not determining in detail the linguistic or conceptual content of what happens. In terms of all our previous discussion, the syllabus now is a syllabus with gaps, and the gaps are more important than the syllabus itself. The language work cannot be designed in detail, because the syllabus being developed will be that of the learner, not the teacher: the syllabus designer provides, and structures the major part of the input but the learner structures the whole of the learning. A communicative methodology will be a methodology that allows the learner to do this, without losing the advantages of the greater experience of language learning situations which good teachers bring to the classroom. We should now turn away from syllabus definition, and look more systematically at communicative methodology.

Notional Syllabuses Revisited:
a response to Wilkins on notional syllabuses

(from *Applied Linguistics*, **2**, 1, 1981)

It may be helpful, before commenting directly on Wilkins's position, to distinguish a number of different aspects of syllabus organization. By syllabus organization I mean the whole process of organizing and specifying what is to be taught in a body of materials, or in an educational institution, in order to enable the learning of a language to be as effective as possible.

First, a syllabus must be goal-directed. Its main justification is that it enables a learner to achieve certain objectives—that is why learners pay money, or governments make education compulsory, because they believe that experience of an organized educational process enables learning to occur more effectively than through disorganized experience. A syllabus is that organization made explicit so that we can discuss it and improve it.

Second, since a syllabus implies movement, it must contain a starting point as well as an end point. The starting point must relate to learner behaviour, for whatever the goals of the syllabus are, work can only start from where the learner is at the time of entry.

Third, a syllabus is an administrative tool; that is, it is a device which has to operate in the real world of institutions and commerce. A syllabus which is effective will need to be as securely based in actual institutions or behaviour patterns as a bridge is in actual solid ground.

Fourth, a syllabus necessarily involves us in making generalizations, for it is—directly—a device for teaching with, not for learning from, and teaching is rarely addressed to individuals. Syllabuses are aimed at classes in schools, at hypothetical learners in textbooks or teach yourself books, and the goals, and the learner behaviour will necessarily be generalized in the syllabus specification. A syllabus specifies a way of offering material to people, so that they may take it up: it cannot specify precisely *how* they take it up, because each person has slightly different needs, motivation and learning style, and because each person varies in commitment to learning from lesson to lesson.

Fifth, none of the above comments in themselves imply a principle of organization. They tell us what a syllabus is for, what it has to do, but the internal organization of a syllabus, while it must be compatible with the demands of the four points above, must be responsible to quite other considerations. Let us briefly consider what those are.

Principles for internal organization will be either intrinsic or extrinsic. Intrinsic cohesion will be dependent on the extent to which items in the syllabus are elements of a system. If they are, then it will be possible to present the system in a structured way so that the overall system is reflected in the organization and sequencing of the elements. A justification for such an organization will rest on the claim that we learn by systematizing, that we are naturally programmed to establish order and that we are more likely to learn effectively what can be perceived as a system than what can only be perceived as unrelated items. Such a claim has strong support in learning theory.

However, extrinsic criteria may also have to be produced for a language learning syllabus. These are criteria, usually defended on motivational grounds, in which an apparent cohesion may be established by the introduction of a story line, for example, in a text, or by the inclusion of information thought to be attractive to students. Such stories or information will not be essential to the presentation of the material, but they will allow an externally imposed pattern to attract learners, in order to introduce them to the hard core of what needs to be taught without alienating them unduly. It should be noted, finally, that extrinsic criteria may be called in either because the stark system of the intrinsic organization is forbiddingly arid and dense, or because a series of disparate elements are being taught which have to be given the illusion of organization by an externally imposed pattern. Syllabuses, including language syllabuses, are the products of tradition, and may well conventionally include a whole range of elements which cannot and should not be reduced to one specific system. The appearance of cohesion may only be achieved by means of external packaging.

Whatever criteria we use, however, and syllabuses inevitably find themselves using a mixture of the two types, principles of organization must be answerable to a view of how language is learnt. It is on the basis of a view of the nature of language learning that systematizability and motivation are seen as important criteria for the selection and ordering of items.

*   *   *   *   *

Since Wilkins, in neither his book (1976) nor in Notional Syllabuses Revisited (1981), addresses himself to learning theory, it is difficult to see on what grounds he really proposes his reorientation. He could be proposing a different goal—'not structures but notions'—but this would only be a justifiable position if earlier theorists had claimed that we learn grammar as *grammar*, and it is clear that grammar has always been seen as a means to a communicative end. Perhaps he is proposing notions and functions not as goals, but as principles of organization. But here we need to be careful. If they are being suggested as principles for internal cohesion, then we need a strong theoretical justification. If they are being suggested as principles for extrinsic cohesion, then he is not really suggesting that something different should be taught, but simply that a different kind of cloak should be laid over the grammar. And indeed this is the way in which a number of textbooks have treated functions and notions, as an external device, rather like a story line, for the establishment of dialogues and communicative activities. Let us assume, though, that Wilkins is making the strong claim, that notions establish a fundamental organizing principle for the language system that has to be mastered. What sort of a claim is this?

First, it entails a view that notions are definable and that the relations between them are specifiable. We know that notions are meaning elements, and in NS there is the beginning of a taxonomy. But it is by no means clear how we could go about falsifying a particular list of notions. Yet we cannot build a serious structure out of a series of categories which can be plucked out of the air. Just to take a few of the problems: do these meaning elements derive from the language system, as with case relations, or do they move out into the real world, involving us in disputes about interpretation versus intention? Should we, as van Ek appears to, chase off into the by-ways of vocabulary in our pursuit of notions (in which case is the list of notions infinitely expandable, like the lexicon, and what does that imply for the system?), or should we restrict ourselves to formal semantic relations (within, beyond? the sentence)? If notions include 'categories of communicative function', have we a list which is in principle infinite, because there are as many ways of doing things with language as people can invent? Or are we simply talking about speech acts, which can be specified fairly economically in terms of knowledge of the world? Or perhaps we are simply talking about *conventionalized* speech acts? Whatever it is is unclear. But until we have some way of saying 'X is a notion and Y is not, and we can test them in the following ways', we are talking about a vacuous concept.

Second, it entails a claim that learning a language in some sense requires learning notions rather than learning—say—structures or situations or sounds. It is easy to show (as Wilkins has done) that learning a language is not learning situations. Nor would he deny that grammar and sound systems need to be learnt. But a proposal for a *notional syllabus* implies that something more important is being asserted, that a notional organization is in some sense more fundamental, more profound than other types of organization. The appeal here is made to goals, and learner motivation. But as I tried to show at the beginning, such appeals are insufficient to establish a claim as a major organizing principle. Without being clearer about what exactly a notion should be, it is difficult to assess the claim that learning a language is learning notions, but it is possible to sniff a worrying Whorfianism. If cultural and linguistic meaning is customarily negotiated between users of the language, is there not more sense in providing learners with the tools for negotiation, and the opportunity to practise with them, rather than teaching what they can/should do/mean with those tools? We can generalize to some extent about grammar and pronunciation, but—precisely because these are the purposes for which people want language—we cannot generalize helpfully about what they should do and mean, except by providing information which is theoretically trivial and incapable of systematization. Even if we accept (I do not) that there is a 'tendency of a structural approach to defer effective communicative ability until the later stages of language learning', there is a methodological solution available which does not require a notional or functional organization, however these are defined.

Establishing the effectiveness of a syllabus is partly a pragmatic task, but it requires serious discussion as well. The discussion initiated by Wilkins, and carried on over the last decade, has been extremely valuable. But it seems to me that it has gone as far as it can go at the moment. Syllabuses are concerned with *enabling* people to do things, not with doing things. Goal discussion takes us too glibly into the belief that a list of things to do is a syllabus. It is not. It may have some value in certain LSP situations, but these are not the most desirable educational situations, for they close rather than open doors, they claim short cuts where they cannot justifiably be claimed, and they predict what cannot truthfully be predicted. Only when we can produce a description of language behaviour and language learning which is comprehensively psychosocial will it be worth reopening the debate. If that (perhaps reductionist) goal is ever reached, we shall have the basis for an organizing principle which can be married to our understanding of language learning. But that time is not yet.

Methodological Solutions to the Problems of Communicative Teaching

(a paper given at TESOL Detroit, 1981, and published in Hines and Rutherford (eds.), *On TESOL '81*, Georgetown, TESOL)

Objections to traditional syllabuses

The last decade has seen the establishment of a consensus about what was wrong with grammatical syllabuses. Representative writers (van Ek, 1975; Wilkins, 1976; Widdowson, 1978) have advanced the view that grammatical syllabuses can only offer at best a partial account of language learning with varying degrees of sophistication. The argument, which is a strong one, goes something like this.

Grammar is a specification of the structure of a language. Learners need the language, not in order to display their knowledge of its organization, but in order to perform speech acts and to convey meanings. Furthermore, they themselves recognize this, so they will probably be more motivated to follow a syllabus which stresses performance and meaning rather than structure. Specifying a syllabus in grammatical terms is likely to lead to teachers ploughing their way systematically through an inventory of grammatical structures, whether or not students need or want them, in the interests of a comprehensive survey of the grammar. Even worse, it is probably going to result in discussion in class of grammatical terminology and an emphasis on the descriptive categories rather than language use itself. Above all, the grammatical syllabus concentrates on the organization of the language at the expense of the value of linguistic items in the operation of normal discourse. Grammar is a feature of linguistic competence, but we should be concerned with the rules of use specified by descriptions of communicative competence.

I shall be arguing in this paper that the position outlined above is legitimate insofar as it discusses syllabuses, but misleading in its relations to teaching. The elegance of the competence/communicative competence distinction has distracted our attention from the inelegant, untidier, but much more important matter of relations between teaching and syllabus specifications.

But it should be made clear at the outset that this argument is not an attack in principle on the kind of speculation which resulted in the present consensus. It is essential that speculation continue, for it is only by such attempts to assess the significance of research and theory that we shall perceive possible directions for the improvement of our practice. But such speculation, however rigorously argued, must not be confused with empirical advance. A claim that a particular approach would be interesting to pursue must not be confused with a claim that the approach should be adopted on a large scale. In this paper I shall be concerned with defining ways in which the aims of communicative teaching can be realized in classes as they actually are throughout the world, with all the administrative and professional difficulties that have to be coped with. Insofar as I shall use general categories, these will be categories that may be helpful to teachers thinking about their day-to-day work, rather than ones with a purity which depends on their role in a rigorous logical argument. This is not to dodge logical argument, but simply to insist during this discussion on categories which are useful even if rough, rather than tidy but comprehensible only to those—a small minority of teachers—who read the professional journals.

Traditional syllabuses, then, have often been specified in terms of grammar (and usually lists of words and phonological patterns as well). They have not, until recently, been specified in terms of the acts to be performed in English, and I have still to see a syllabus which really seriously attempts to specify semantic units. The reason for this limitation has had partly to do with the state of linguistic theory, and partly to do with the recognized function of a syllabus. Certainly linguists were far more concerned with the specification of a generalized linguistic knowledge than with rules of use, but this is not to say that teachers were not concerned with teaching the use of the language. The argument was about how best to do this rather than whether to do it. The tacit assumption (and one which still underlies most foreign language teaching) was that first we should teach the code, and that classroom activity would give enough experience of using the code to enable learners to operate on their own when necessary. This was 'skill-using' following 'skill-getting' in Wilga Rivers' terms (Rivers, 1972: 22). The job of the syllabus was to specify what the underlying knowledge of the code to be acquired was before it could be put into use. Syllabus specifications were aimed at teachers' 'presentation' techniques, and provided the content for presentation. During the later 'practice' and 'production' stages the techniques used would assist learners in developing capacities to use the language, but this was a matter for methodology, not for syllabus specification. Thus methodological discussion for many years insisted on the need to 'situationalize' language, to practice it 'in context', and to 'make it meaningful' to the students. Only in recent years has it been claimed that syllabuses should specify the nature of situations, contexts and meaning, and this claim has been a direct result of theoretical speculation, and empirical investigation about the ways in which we behave, in relation to each other, with language.

But there is a problem here. A syllabus is not a device for the description of language; it is a device to assist effective teaching. Indeed, many of the difficulties which have arisen in argument are the result of confusion over what exactly a syllabus is, or what it is meant to do. I have attempted elsewhere to define a syllabus as an administrative tool which involves generalizing about the nature of learning, and specifies a progression from a position where the learner is presumed to be to a stated set of appropriate goals (Brumfit, 1981a). If this view, which does not need to be spelled out in detail here, is accepted, then the structure of a syllabus must be at least partly dependent on a learning theory. This raises problems, particularly if communicative syllabuses are viewed as necessarily notional or functional, for it is difficult to see how such ill-defined categories can be fitted into a view of how language is learned. Until we are able to clarify what the exact status of either a notion or a function is, beyond simply saying that one is an element of meaning and the other a categorization of what we do with language, we cannot see whether they are items in a system. If they are not items in a system, then we may reasonably assume that when we learn whatever it is they represent we are associating that with some other completely different system, perhaps even a grammatical one. For we do know that there is a relatively coherent, economically describable, grammatical system. We have no such knowledge about functions, notions, problem-solving operations, discourse strategies, or any of the other possibilities.

This is to argue that the kind of economical specification of language which teachers (not learners, please note) need cannot as yet be achieved in terms of the communicative categories which are frequently passed around in conferences and seminars. The value of such discussion must remain speculative rather than concrete for most teachers, its main function to provide the guidelines for careful and extremely limited experimentation until such experimentation, and further discussion, enables us to produce something more workable.

Why, then, should a proposal whose 'generalizability remains to be shown . . . lacking in linguistic detail and therefore no more than suggestive (Wilkins, 1974: 91) have achieved such rapid popularity? One reason, of course, was that it was an intellectually exciting proposal which was intuitively attractive. Another was that the language teaching profession is always looking for panaceas to hide from itself, cynics would say, the unpalatable truth that language learning is always nasty, brutish, and long. But underlying any enthusiastic response was, I suggest, a misunderstanding of the nature of teaching, and an assumption that in some way teaching must be subservient to external disciplines, that it has no knowledge of its own. Let me try to clarify this claim by means of a simple diagram.

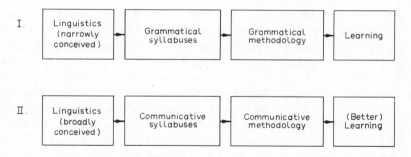

Sequence I represents a reasonable view of the relationship between descriptive linguistics and language teaching in the past. Sequence II represents the view that many people have had of the analogous relationships in more recent times. But to accept such a view is to misunderstand the role of methodology. The function of teaching has always been to take the linguistic core, ensure that it is presented as appropriately as possible, and to establish the conditions for its effective use by learners. Of course over the years there have been changes in the needs that learners have had, the relative importance of reading, or of literature, or of casual conversation has varied, and there have been changes in our understanding of the nature of learning, but teaching methods have always been concerned with enabling learners to use the target language effectively. After all, even learning to read and translate is learning to operate communicatively. It may be true that linguistics has swung back closer to the interests of, say, Sapir or Firth than was customary fifteen years ago, but that is no reason to insist on the narrowness of language teaching methodology. Indeed, in many respects traditional language syllabuses, with their insistence on integrative activities like reading and translation, and their concern with literary content, were more truly communicative than some contemporary ones. The point is that descriptive linguistics has indeed something to offer to syllabus specification, but the syllabus cannot specify the nature of teaching itself. It may be able to offer helpful guidelines, but in the last resort only the teacher, by interacting with the class, can create the activities and environment to enable linguistic specifications to be converted to language use. Language use is performed by people, and emerges from relationships between people. And to describe language use is neither to learn it nor to teach it.

What linguistics, broadly conceived, is doing is to describe and attempt to analyse many things that teachers, through their methodology, and of course all language users through their interaction with each other, have always been doing. If there is to be a development in methodology, it should develop as much out of earlier methodology as out of new syllabus ideas. Knowing how to teach is not the same thing as describing languages, but it is a great deal more important for language teachers, and it is a kind of knowledge, like knowing how to act, or to swim, or to be a good friend, that is learned by being felt and experienced as much as by being described.

Communicative methodology

If teachers have always been concerned with communication, it may be asked, why should there be any change in methodology? One answer is to say that methodology is a product of relationships between teacher and taught, and that if new populations of students emerge, with different expectations and slightly different needs, new methodological principles will necessarily develop. It is more helpful, however, to point out that the reaction to proposals for new communicative syllabuses indicates a great deal of dissatisfaction with existing teaching, and—if methodology is as important as I have claimed—it must be included in the indictment. However, it is important that we ask the right questions. Teaching is not like a science. Science is concerned with solving problems which develop out of earlier problems. Because of this it is possible to talk about the development of science in terms of intellectual advances. But to ask whether languages are better or worse taught now than they used to be is like asking whether marriages are better or worse than they were. There are so many external influences on attitudes, so many close personal factors, and there is so little clear understanding of what is involved, that general comments are impossible to evaluate. We can try to improve, but we would be unwise, on the basis of past experience, to expect to discover any all-purpose formula. Yet we can benefit from sources very little tapped, the experience of teachers themselves, of students themselves, in normal classrooms, operating competently without the benefit of the amazing breakthrough, the latest 'method' or the master teacher. This is where most successful, as well as most unsuccessful teaching takes place, and it is within such ordinary surroundings that any substantial improvement will have to occur.

Teachers can control the methods they use; they can control little else. Yet changes made to materials or syllabuses will be ineffective if teachers fail to understand them or feel unconvinced of the need for change. Furthermore, teachers do know and understand methodology. That is what they are planning when they think ahead about their work; that is what they are improvising with as they adapt their preparation to their classes. Any serious improvement to teaching must be based on teachers. So any categories for discussion that we use must be sufficiently simple to be interpreted by teachers of all kinds, native and nonnative speakers, trained and untrained, lazy and committed, those who would not be seen dead at a TESOL conference as well as those who are already planning for the next.

Yet how are we to find categories which will genuinely influence teaching procedures in desirable directions, and be compatible with the changes which all of us accept as intellectually convincing? One way is to look for categories which reflect changes in our attitude to language acquisition procedures. Recent emphasis, from a wide range of sources, on the integration of language use and language acquisition (Halliday, 1975), on acquisition rather than overt learning (Krashen, 1976), on the role of error and simplification (Corder, 1978), and on the involvement of student personality (Stevick, 1976; Moskowitz, 1978) tends to demand some sharp distinction between the traditional emphasis on skill-getting and a modern emphasis on skill-using. Only the term 'skill' is unfortunate and is best avoided. But one basic point which needs to be emphasized in any discussion of teaching is the role of 'natural' language activity, whether conversation, writing or reading.

A convenient pair of terms to express this distinction without introducing unnecessary technicality is *accuracy* and *fluency*. In many ways of course it does not matter exactly which terms are chosen as long as the distinction is made clear, but it helps to use terms which are available in normal usage, as long as we are not insisting on complexities of exact definitions. These terms are memorable enough and meaningful enough for our purposes.

The convenience of such a binary distinction is that it is simple, and corresponds to basic planning elements in any teacher's activity. Some work, we can say, must be aimed at accuracy, and some at fluency. And we can further point out that syllabuses specify what has to be introduced to the students, by means of accuracy work, but that far more time is necessary for students to spend on fluency work, in the course of which they will internalize items to which they have only previously been exposed. To put it in more sophisticated terms, accuracy work requires operation of the monitor; fluency work presumably assists acquisition, in Krashen's model. Learning how to mean, in Halliday's model, will emerge primarily through fluency work, but accuracy work will enable the tokens with which meaning is negotiated to be made available to the nonnative speaker.

Fluency work, then, occurs whenever the student, with whatever inadequate dialect has so far been internalized, behaves like a native speaker, and consequently is using language without fear of correction, but with a concern for the message or the purpose of language use. But fluency work will still be dependent on the provision of some amount of accuracy work. There will be many occasions when students will want to be corrected, and when they should expect presentation by the teacher of new items, and here accuracy is the issue, but this must not be confused with the learning process itself. That can only occur when students themselves operate the language, for their own purposes—though often guided by the teacher—and, more importantly, in their own way.

My experience of discussing this distinction with teachers on many occasions is that they find it intuitively helpful, and not so radical as to alienate the conservative, nor so reactionary as to alienate the radical.

But having made the distinction, the crucial issue remains of what is to be done with it. It does enable us immediately to ask teachers to assess what proportion of class time has recently been spent on fluency work, and to suggest, if necessary and it usually is, that a much greater proportion of fluency activity is desirable. The problem is that syllabuses and course books usually measure teaching, not learning, by specifying what the teacher must do and not indicating the gaps or holes in the syllabus during which student activity, and consequently student learning, is greatest. If we offer a rule of thumb (a minimum of one third of the time at the very beginning, rising to upwards of ninety percent on fluency work) we can at least orientate teachers towards procedures which reduce the learning load and increase acquisition chances. Furthermore, procedures for the development of fluency activities do not require massive new doses of materials into exhausted educational systems. All textbooks can be worked on in groups, for any kind of exercise, and discussion can be moved towards English, even if a pidgin English, from an early stage. There are, of course, many books of communication games which can be drawn upon for assistance (e.g. Maley and Duff, 1978), but teachers do not have to depend on these. Certainly, teacher training courses need to sensitize trainees to this distinction, and to spend a great deal of time on helping them to use existing materials for fluency activity.

Simple but useful categories such as these will enable teachers to concentrate primarily on what they do in class rather than on the syllabus specifications. In this way the emphasis in teaching will be on the process of teaching, and innovation will be centred on the people, teachers, and the place, the classroom, where it can expect to be genuinely effective. To give the responsibility for innovation to other experts, however competent and committed they may be, is to remove it from the one group of people who can adapt change sensitively to the precise needs of the learners whom they serve and the society in which they work.

Some Humanistic Doubts about Humanistic Language Teaching

(from *ELT Documents 113*, 1982, The British Council)

'Humanistic' is a good thing to be. The literature both in psychology and language teaching makes it clear that no sensible person should want to be anti-humanistic. Humanistic teachers do many things which pre-humanistic teachers considered desirable. Unlike their opponents, humanistic teachers see language as something which must engage the whole person, not as something purely intellectual; they recognize that their students are people like themselves, with emotional and spiritual needs as well as intellectual ones, people who can contribute to their own learning, who are not the passive recipients of someone else's teaching; humanistic teachers believe in a world of autonomous, creative and emotionally secure people, and they believe that education can assist the process of creating such a world.

Such claims, which can be gathered, explicitly and implicitly, from the works of Stevick, Moskowitz, Simon *et al.*, Gattegno, Curran and many others, are immediately attractive, but they are also very general. Throughout much discussion of humanistic teaching there is an implicit opponent, but it is difficult to work out who it is—for we are all on the side of virtue. In postwar Western society it would be difficult to find many teachers who would not subscribe to the humanistic ideals. Argument is only likely to arise when we start discussing the most appropriate means of achieving these goals, and the role of the teacher in this process.

It is important to make this point right at the beginning, for there is a tendency in casual discussion of humanistic teaching to see the pursuit of virtuous goals as uniquely embedded in a given set of procedures. Statements of concern for the complexities of learners, which have been received with delight and appreciation in language teaching circles, are very often no more than contemporary rephrasings of basic axioms in traditional general teacher training. This is true to such a great extent that one wonders whether much humanistic discussion is simply a reflection of the fact that—unlike almost any other area of basic teaching—language teaching can be entered with little or no educational training. In some ways it is embarrassing to be a member of a profession in which so many people are so totally unaware of the basic approaches to learning, classrooms and learners that all primary school teachers are exposed to during their three years of training. One fact in particular needs to be emphasized: there can be no instant solutions, for human beings are so infinitely complex that teachers must be infinitely sensitive to their students' variabilities. And there is no method, and no book, which can be a substitute for the guidance of another experienced teacher and the experience of actually working a normal teaching life. Being a good teacher means enabling students to learn, and there are as many ways of doing that as there are teachers and students.

But this is only to attack the misuse of humanistic discussion. Books may offer us guidance from experienced teachers, and the best of the books in the humanistic tradition (Stevick, 1976 and 1980, for example) have value precisely because they enable us to watch experienced teachers grappling with problems central to their professional life in the light of their own reading and discussions with other teachers. Even more dogmatic and tendentious books will provide us with stimulation by virtue of their very dogmatism. But there are more central issues which we should be wary of, and these do deserve more extended discussion.

Teaching and therapy

One aspect of humanistic teaching derives from a therapeutic tradition. This tradition is influential in a number of ways: directly, in Curran's work with Counselling Learning (Curran, 1976); in Moskowitz's work (Moskowitz, 1978); through Stevick's interest in transactional analysis (Stevick, 1976). This tradition relates teaching to the work of Rogers (1969) and to a movement in self-education which developed, particularly through encounter groups in the States, to have a momentum of its own independent of, and to some extent in opposition to, the conventional education system.

A number of commentators (e.g. Kovel, 1976) have described how humanistic psychology has emerged from a philosophical basis in existentialism, with its emphasis on alienation. In opposition to the expertise of the Freudian or Jungian expert figure, the therapist and the patient start from their equal need for shared experience in the present. The opposite of alienation is contact, which happens in the present. Explanation and understanding are products of the past, and depend on expertise, on diagnosis of cause and effect, but contact can be achieved through an immediate relationship with the therapist without the barrier created by expertise.

This is of course a condensed summary of a complex position, and is therefore bound to be unfair. But it is possible to comment on some of the risks when a model such as this is applied to education. There are major difficulties with transferring ideas from medical to non-medical domains. Psychiatrists and doctors habitually see people who have defined themselves as so deviant as to require attention. Techniques which have been devised to cope with breakdown are concerned with returning individuals to normal mental or physical life as far as possible. But 'normal' life encompasses an enormous range of states of mental and physical activity. There are major ethical questions relating to the classification of people as mental patients anyway, but these questions become even stronger if we are going to imply that mental health is in some sense an absolute. Common sense forces us to admit that some modes of behaviour are so embarrassing, or so anti-social, or so dangerous that they need to be adjusted to enable the patient to survive in society. But such a view, even if we regard behaviour as operating on a cline from mediocre normality to spectacular idiocy, does not require that we insist on public behaviour converging on a set of preconceived patterns of well-adjustment. It may be one of the functions of schools to detect deviance that is likely to be dangerous; it is not one of the functions to prevent deviance that is *not* likely to be dangerous. Indeed, we might want to argue that schools should be in the business of creating (fruitful) deviance.

There are occasions when teachers have to deal with anti-social and dangerously deviant behaviour and it would be ridiculous to argue that they should not be equipped to do this effectively. But within the boundaries of socially acceptable behaviour, there must be a wide freedom of choice available to students. And this is particularly important in language work. We may accept Stevick's arguments (1976) about the necessity to help learners to use language as deeply and realistically as possible, but this need not lead us to the position of Moskowitz that learning will benefit from students having wholesome relationships with classmates. It is not only that much learning, understanding and discovery seems to have emerged from distinctly unwholesome rivalries and jealousies in the past (see, for example, Watson, 1968), but also that we cannot define a 'wholesome' relationship —they come in infinite varieties and our responsibility must be limited to discouraging unwholesome ones. To illustrate one aspect of this argument, let us consider an exercise in Moskowitz, 1978 (p.93). The exercise is called 'I Like You—You're Different', and the affective purposes of the exercise are listed as:

> 'To encourage students to feel proud of their differences rather than feeling the need to be conformists
> To encourage an open attitude toward others and their differences'.

The basic procedure is given as follows:

> 'Before giving the assignment, introduce the activity as follows:
> "Very often we feel it's important to be like other people, and we worry if we feel that we're different. At times it's fine to be like others, but it's also important to accept and be proud of our differences. There are many ways that we are like each other in this class, but there are also things about us that are not true of anyone else in this class.
> "For tomorrow write down on a card three things you feel good about that make you different from everyone else in the class. That is, they are not true of anyone else here." . . .
> Tell the students to write their names on the cards turned in and not to tell anyone what they wrote. Announce that you will collect the cards and read them aloud, and that they will guess the identity of the people.'

Let us first be clear that this procedure, with an experienced and sympathetic teacher, could produce an exciting lesson. This is not the point at issue. What is important is whether the structure is misleading in terms of its own affective purposes, and whether these purposes are themselves undesirable. First, we may ask whether there is not a basic confusion between what we make public and what we keep private in our lives. 'Feeling proud' is not (if the words are intended to be taken seriously) something which we normally express overtly and publicly. Furthermore, we shall, if we are at all sensitive, feel proud of some of our differences and ashamed of some others; indeed we may not be sure which we should be proud of and which ashamed of. If humanistic education is really concerned with feelings like pride, self-image, etc., then it must consider them with more subtlety than in this example. There is here a direct conflict between the public mode of the classroom and the private individuality of the deep feelings which are being referred to so glibly. The experienced teacher may use this to create an exciting lesson by specifically pushing the differences towards the socially acceptable ones which can be made public and by tacitly discouraging those which are causes of genuine internal conflict to individual students. To do the opposite, and cause a student to make public, in a classroom setting, what is intimate and worrying, is to break down inhibitions in a way that may be necessary for a therapist dealing with extreme cases of mental disturbance, but which is quite inappropriate with a presumably normal student. And anyway, teachers do not have the expertise, experience and training to deal with such public avowals of private tensions. No doubt students are able to distance themselves from such intrusions adequately, but it is important to note that the procedure cannot have any genuine relationship with the avowed purposes, because the procedure is public and pedagogic, and any concern with the stated purposes in education can only be indirect.

An affectively-based methodology

We do not need to talk about affective variables all the time in order to include them in our methodology. Nor do we need an analysis of affective variables in order to build it into our syllabuses.

The first principle of any genuine relationship between human beings should be that of mutual respect, and this entails accepting the other members of the group as what they are, and leaving them with the freedom to be what they are. An affectively-based methodology needs to be based in part on a classroom organization which is sufficiently free to enable students to make their own initiatives on their own terms in any matters which relate to their deeper feelings. If they wish to talk about political or personal issues they, like any other persons, should be free to negotiate the terms on which they will do it. But it must be recognized that topics in which there is likely to be considerable ego-involvement cannot be forced on students compulsorily without risking the creation of the alienation that such topics are supposed to be preventing. True affective teaching is far more likely to emerge in the following educational contexts:

1. Those where staff-student contact takes place over a long period so that participants have time to build up a genuine relationship.
2. Those where teachers perform their tasks efficiently but with a consistent regard for the feelings and variable needs of students.
3. Those where there is a great deal of unstructured staff–student contact.
4. Those where the staff are confident of the abilities of students to succeed.
5. Those where students are confident that the staff understand exactly why they are doing what they do.
6. Those where the staff visibly respect each other and work together as a team.

In other words, successful affective teaching is more likely to emerge when students join a community in which they are provided with an example of the desired behaviour patterns than when the patterns are built into some kind of syllabus structure.

But this is not to say that there cannot be a link between syllabus design and the engagement of the student's deepest motivations. Such a link will be established, within the context of the community referred to above, whenever language work is demanded in realistic situations within the classroom—that is, whenever fluency activity takes place (Brumfit, 1980b). The whole point about fluency activities is that they allow the initiative within the context of the exercise, to remain with the students, who can decide how much or how little to contribute of themselves. Those who wish to remain inhibited can remain so, those who wish to be extrovert can be so, but the coercion of the educational structure is minimized by the methodology, not diverted to the affective domain.

To summarize: the point about an affective education is that the teacher should know what is undesirable behaviour at the extremes, but should *not* know precisely what should be desirable behaviour. Affective education should be built on a methodology for freedom, not on a set of affective purposes.

The humanistic paradox

Humanistic psychology and education are both committed to two propositions which make description and discussion difficult. These propositions are that the starting point should be human experience, and that humanity is essentially whole, the human experience cannot usefully be divided into discrete parts. Such propositions are a convenient corrective to the tendency to see human beings as bundles of isolated features, but they remain elusive when described in print, for the written mode necessarily consists of a sequence of separate sentences. One result of this is that descriptions of what to do in humanistic teaching may easily be converted into sets of separate instructions, and thus lose their wholeness and integrity. Another is that description of humanistic experiences may pose problems which may not arise for people working in more analytic traditions. Stevick (1980) has attempted to avoid this difficulty by deliberately approaching his record of personal experiences through a variety of devices—essays, poems, views of his own activity from other people, and so on. Because the viewpoint changes, and the emphasis shifts from intellectual to affective in different parts of the book, the picture may be more complete than in—for example—the consistent expository prose of *Memory, Meaning and Method* (Stevick, 1976). But the earlier book has one important merit, compared with the later, which is that it is possible to argue with it. It is of course possible to argue with parts of the latter book, but as a whole we can only agree with the experience, or not—on the basis of its closeness to our own needs and expectations—just as we do with a novel. In part, the two books can be seen as examples, within the same tradition, of first the rational and then the experiential mode of communication. Both undoubtedly have value, and they are in no sense mutually exclusive, but there are some arguments for considering the rational mode as more important in discussion of teaching. These arguments are particularly significant since humanistic teaching seems to attract those who are disposed to reject analytical modes of argument as dry, academic and inhumane. This line of reasoning (or unreasoning) is wrong at a fundamental level, and it seems worthwhile to spell out the reasons for it being wrong.

A defence of reason in a humanistic context

Teaching is an art in which the relationship between human beings, between teacher and taught, is crucial to real success. This is one way of distinguishing teaching from training, for the latter can be successful simply via a series of instructions, but the former, necessarily involving basic moral and psychological issues, engages the whole persons of both teachers and learners. However, having said this, it is difficult to add a great deal that is illuminating to those who have not experienced teaching already. Learning to teach is not to pick up formulae but to act on internalized principles—to borrow terminology from religious instruction, we are concerned not with outward and visible signs, but with inward and spiritual graces. The signs are the conventions of particular times and places, but the internal motivation and sensitivity of the good teacher will transcend the limitations of particular local conventions through the process of relating to people—the class. Each teacher re-creates the principles of teaching in relation to each new class and each new student. Some teachers do it better than others, of course, but all teachers will attest to gradually getting a 'feel' for teaching as they become more experienced. We can analyse this feeling, but the analysis will not lead to experience—it must come after the event—and the event can only occur in the process of teaching. Analysis concerns itself with facts; teaching 'feel' is concerned with values. The values are the most important aspect of teaching, but in the public domain we only have facts available for scrutiny, for we cannot live values in print, we can only refer to them, and careful reference turns rapidly to analysis.

Because of this, it is dangerous to assume that intellectual analysis and description of events can be a substitute for experience. But it is equally dangerous to assume that experience, however sensitive, can be a substitute for analysis. We have no procedure other than analysis for checking that our subjectively-perceived experiences tally with those of other people, and there are plenty of examples of well-meaning subjective experiences turning into horrifying objective ones. Any of us who work in service professions, especially when we are involved with young people, have a particular responsibility to monitor our own activities all the time, and always to be suspicious of our own beliefs and motives. Only by constantly testing our assumptions and principles against the ideas of other people, only by making these assumptions and principles as explicit as possible so that other people can tear them to pieces, can we avoid the risk of exploiting our students and colleagues, or worse still, of harming them unintentionally. Any movement which over-emphasizes experience risks degenerating towards moral chaos, for there are no shared safeguards (if this is doubted, Blumberg and Golembiewski, 1976, on the encounter group movement should be consulted). Perhaps before Stalin and Hitler romantic naivety was forgivable, but the price of liberty now must be constant suspicion, and we cannot afford to rely on intuitive experience—not because it is less reliable than publicly reasoned discussion, but because its workings cannot by definition be publicly scrutinized. Rational criticism can be used to evil ends, but it is accessible and no other basis for belief is.

Criticism must be responsible. We should make the maximum effort to understand what we criticize; we must be willing to have our minds changed; we must couch criticisms in forms that can be falsified; we must assist our opponents to attack our views by always being willing to continue the argument. But only by doing this can we prevent ourselves slipping imperceptibly into a commitment which cannot be rationally justified, and there is then no way of distinguishing a good from a bad commitment. By acting like this we lose something—spontaneity, innocence, the willingness to act instinctively—but we do gain responsibility and we diminish risk. Knowing twentieth-century power and twentieth-century history as we do, we cannot responsibly accept moral risks, however attractive the alleged gain.

This discussion has not related language teaching to our deepest impulses. Language teaching is—numerically—a mass movement, and any mass movement related to our deepest impulses is to be feared and dreaded. It has related language teaching to some important issues which will not disappear. Whether or not this approach, which derives mainly from the views of Popper (see for example, Popper, 1972, 1976), can be called humanistic is for the reader to judge. But whatever we call it, humanity needs it.

Alternative Language-teaching Strategies and Conventional Education

(paper given at the Paris Colloquium, September 1982, and published in
Triangle **2**, 1982, Paris)

It will not have escaped the notice of most observers of humanistic educational discussion that language teaching packages are not a British, nor—with the exception of Suggestopaedia—a continental European phenomenon. Yet it would certainly be justified to assert that European creativity and innovation have not been lacking in the decade during which 'alternative' approaches have become popular. We have only to think of the work of the Council of Europe (for example, Coste *et al*, 1976; Richterich and Chancerel, 1977), of CRAPEL, of individuals such as Corder (1981), Widdowson (1978, 1979) and Wilkins (1976) in Britain, or of the various proceedings of the Neuchâtel/Berne colloquia in applied linguistics, to recognize that Europe has been a fecund source of ideas and innovation. Even materials writers who share a great deal with the humanistic tradition (such as Maley and Duff, 1978) have been content to offer their work as resources for teachers to call upon within a general educational tradition. But what has been in practice a strong transatlantic phenomenon has been a method attached to a guru: Asher's *Direct Physical Response*, Gattegno's *The Silent Way*, Curran's *Counselling Learning*, Lozanov's *Suggestopaedia*, Terrell's (or perhaps Krashen's) *Natural Method*. Even when the originator is not himself transatlantic, the publicity and development usually is.

There has of course at the same time been a mainstream American tradition, represented most conspicuously by Rivers and Finocchiaro, which observes alternative strategies and attempts to relate them to the central tradition in the same way that many European commentators have done, and there are also writers like Moskowitz (1976) and Stevick (1976, 1980) who, like Maley, exploit humanistic ideas without attempting to sell a package. But packages are a recognizable phenomenon, and they have a certain appeal. It is the purpose of this paper to argue that packages are dangerous, and that we in Europe should hold fast to our tradition of scepticism—though I hope to do this in a way which avoids possible charges of complacency or conservatism.

We do of course argue retrospectively about language teaching approaches, using for simplicity terms like 'direct method', 'grammar-translation method' and so on. But we need to recognize that such terms make sense as descriptions of movements after the event, as generalizations about the development of language teaching—though, like any historical generalization, they can be dangerous if taken too literally. When we are offered generalizations in advance, we seem to be getting something closer to a marketing principle than to serious analysis. And marketing and scientific understanding do not mix.

Language teaching history abounds in methods. At the age of nineteen John Stuart Mill was learning German by the Hamiltonian method (Mill, 1873: 83), and language schools such as Berlitz have been founded on successful accumulations of techniques. No serious student of language learning or teaching can afford to ignore them. Nor should we either write off alternative language teaching strategies as eccentric and therefore useless, or refuse to sample them actively as teachers and learners. But the questions we need to ask about any global package are only two:

(i) What aspects of the package contribute to its 'success'?
(ii) To what extent is mainstream teaching deficient in these aspects, so that teachers and students are attracted by such a package?

To justify such a claim I need to outline a view of the nature of language teaching.

I believe that language and language teaching and learning are complex and little understood phenomena. I also believe that, while we have a responsibility to understand the underlying processes as fully as we can, we cannot in principle produce a full account of what we want learners to do when they learn a foreign language. This is not simply because language is closely bound up with culture and personality—two massively complex and unsimplifiable concepts—but also because the acquisition of a new language or new dialect opens up possibilities for the user which are literally unpredictable (see Harris, 1980, for a full explication of this argument). Furthermore, language users create their language for their own purposes, insofar as they operate naturally with language, and—except as a facilitating device in pedagogy—we cannot constrain the language taught by attempting to predict how it should be used or what formal features it may possess.

But to say that teaching and learning languages are little understood is not to say that they cannot be done well. We all know many students and teachers who show the extent of possible success. However, we have to be very certain before we can establish exactly what it is about good language teachers or learners that *causes* their success: many learners attribute success to factors which make little sense to experts, or which conflict directly with contemporary pedagogical opinion. The varieties of possible successful language learning strategy have been shown convincingly by Pickett (1978), and the kinds of generalizations that can be conveniently made about good language learners are insufficiently explicit to be used as touchstones for new methods. In a survey of good language learners, Naiman, Fröhlich, Stern and Todesco (1978) revealed five consistent tendencies:

1. The learners must be active in their approach to learning and practice.
2. The learners must come to grips with the language as a system.
3. The learners must use the language in real communication.
4. The learners must monitor their interlanguage.
5. The learners must come to terms with the affective demands of language learning.

(p.103)

While we may want to argue that any method that encourages learners to do all these things successfully will be a good one, we should still recognize that there are further complications. We only have to ask questions like 'How active is "active"?'

or 'What constitutes "real" communication?' to see some of the difficulties. Logically, we must recognize that there are only three necessary conditions for language learning:

1. Learners must be exposed to the target language.
2. They must have opportunities to interact meaningfully with the language.
3. They must be motivated to make use of these opportunities.

Everything else about language learning is *conventional* and consequently negotiable.

But language teaching procedures are themselves changing parts of a total semiotic system operated by teachers. The same technique used today and tomorrow will be different in each case. Once it is new, but the second time it is being repeated. One part of the originality of new ideas is simply their unexpectedness. By definition this originality cannot last for ever. Good teachers learn to surprise their classes; less good teachers, or less experienced teachers, buy their surprises in packages from other people.

Teaching procedures are also more convincing if they reflect current ideas about the nature of language learning, and lead to language work which is compatible with current needs for particular kinds of language. Both the ideas and the needs change as the world changes, and the procedures—if they are to convince students of their relevance and authority—will need to change too. The issue is only partly whether the ideas about language learning are correct, or whether the needs are appropriate; far more it is whether the teacher convinces students that they are. Consequently, Lozanov's concept of authority becomes extremely important. But authority is a product of a relationship between teacher, student and their social environment, and the conventions through which authority is made manifest will have to vary whenever that relationship varies. Techniques appropriate for a highly selective environment, or for a self-selected group of students, or for small groups of adults, will rarely be suitable for mixed ability large groups of adolescents in a compulsory state educational system.

But this does not mean that teachers in the latter situation should be unaware of developments in former situations. Only by the process of piecemeal borrowing from successes (or indeed interesting failures) in other conditions will we innovate and improve in our own classes. What we cannot do, however, is look for a specific and correct answer to the question 'How should I teach languages?' Even modestly presented packages imply that responsibility can be taken away from the teacher and given to the deviser of the package. Indeed the author of the package frequently makes money out of selling faith in a total set of procedures.

But there are some teachers who do need help and support: the inexperienced, those who are unsure of their knowledge of the language they teach—most non-native speakers in practice, those who are overworked. Should we not offer packages to them? Only, I would wish to argue, insofar as the package assists the process of creating an autonomously developing teaching profession. The purpose of a package is to create the rationale for rejecting it and becoming free, though of course only 'free' within the constraints of responsibility to effective language teaching for particular students. Essentially, then, any packaging should be regarded as a teacher training device, a means of providing teachers with security until they are confident enough to create their own styles, independent of textbook, interpreting syllabuses into methodology appropriate for each particular class.

Undoubtedly there are teachers who, having trained for a particular method, work freely and independently in a style which has developed out of the original method. There are others who, like Stevick, adjust their own styles in the light of their reading and experience with newer approaches. There are others, however, who appear to have seen the light, who operate with a messianic fervour in the service of whichever prophet they have chosen to serve. The point at issue here is not whether they teach effectively—messianic fervour may be an effective motivating force. Rather, the point is what effect such fervour has on the profession. Teaching is not simply a science, but it is partly a science, and the responsibility of teachers is not limited to their own classes. Without an atmosphere of enquiry and questioning (the same atmosphere which led the originators of these methods to reject tradition and work out alternative possibilities themselves), the profession will stagnate, becoming simply a collection of sects and cliques, each clinging to its own received truth. We should be working towards an integrated profession, not one which trains for particular methods only (even for the Council of Europe) but for a broad interpretation of all interesting and potentially usable developments. Beneath this view of the teaching profession lies an epistemology and a social philosophy which derives partially from Popper (1957, 1972) and to a lesser extent from his opponent Feyerabend (1975). From Popper comes a view of science and understanding the world as a process based on problem-solving with a permanent policy of open criticism, together with a view of the necessity for piecemeal rather than revolutionary, wholesale reform. Adapting teaching methodology cannot be regarded as the application of ideas from any exact science, whether linguistics or psychology, for reasons deriving from the nature of language outlined above. It is much closer to the implementation of economic or social policies, where Popper's cautious scepticism is entirely appropriate:

> But the only way to apply something like scientific method in politics is to proceed on the assumption that there can be no political move which has no drawbacks, no undesirable consequences. To look out for these mistakes, to find them, to bring them into the open, to analyse them, and to learn from them, this is what a scientific politician as well as a political scientist must do. Scientific method in politics means that the great art of convincing ourselves that we have not made any mistakes, of ignoring them, of hiding them, and of blaming others for them, is replaced by the greater art of accepting the responsibility for them, of trying to learn from them, and of applying this knowledge so that we may avoid them in the future.
>
> (Popper, 1957: 88)

It is particularly this somewhat puritan caution that Feyerabend attacks. But we do not need to accept a full, activist implementation of his avowedly anarchist, even dadaist approach to recognize its value as a useful source of innovation into the more heavily institutionalized profession, represented by government institutions, examination boards, teacher training colleges and even conferences such as this one. We cannot institutionalize anarchy, and a totally uninstitutionalized educational system will directly result in the exploitation of the students; but we can recognize the necessity for exploration and development which can be predicted, neither by bureaucrats nor by scholars. Language is so rich a phenomenon that we cannot encompass it in a prescribed theoretical statement of any specificity. We shall remain permanently surprised by the possibilities in teaching and learning it: no evidence should be alien to us, no procedures rejected on *a priori* grounds.

One of the great challenges posed by the work of many of the less conventional methodologists has not rested so much in their practice as in their willingness to justify language teaching and learning by reference to a more abstract set of assumptions about the complexities of learners, and the nature of understanding, than mainstream education or applied linguistics. If we feel that there are risks as well as gains in this, or if we feel that there are real dangers in some of the underlying assumptions, then we need to respond with an argument at the same level of abstraction, perhaps similar to the one I have sketched here, and developed more explicitly in Brumfit, 1982, rather than assume that our position requires no epistemological justification.

But what of the particular content of new methodologies? What do they offer that accounts for their appeal? Is it merely messianic fervour and somewhat bizarre techniques? If we accept my argument so far, the last question cannot be answered by 'Yes'. But it is in practice very difficult to generalize about the various methodologies usually grouped together. They have very dissimilar origins, and sometimes conflict with each other at crucial points, for example in the explicitness of much Silent Way learning contrasted with the peripheral nature of Suggest-opaedic acquisition. Although it is claimed by supporters that all these methods aim at creating secure conditions for learners, they vary considerably in practical means of achieving such security. Indeed, the founder of one of these popular alternative methods has a casual reputation as a deliberate creator of insecurity among those who participate in demonstrations of his method! Nor can the packaged methods really be compared with each other as attempts to solve essentially the same problem. The Silent Way is an attempt by a maverick educator of undoubted genius to work out a pragmatic series of procedures for enabling certain types of learner to master foreign languages (following similar innovative work in other spheres of education such as mathematics and literacy). Gattegno has remarked in answer to questions that if learners do not like his approach to the class, or the procedures he advocates, they should leave the class and go somewhere else. But there is no question that many learners feel themselves to have benefited from the method. Counselling Learning, on the other hand, is a general approach to teaching, borrowing concepts from psychiatric counselling, which has been adapted to language work by a number of people, using a variety of procedures. Again, many teachers and learners feel that it has been successful, but again it has mainly been used with small groups of highly motivated learners. At first sight there may appear to be major similarities between the emphasis in the Silent Way on independence and autonomy (Gattegno, 1976: 45ff) and that in Counselling on learner responsibility (Curran, 1976: 4-5), but it is clear from the general trend of writings in both areas that Gattegno is more responsive to the learners as consciously setting out to exploit themselves and their will to master the learning materials most effectively, while Curran is more concerned with the needs of both teacher and learner, and the nature of the human relationship in which both are participating. Suggestopaedia, on the other hand, for all its unusual features as a methodology, is much more mainstream intellectually, being part of a general learning theory which developed within the same kind of academic tradition as those of Skinner or Piaget. While Lozanov's work has been severely criticized (Scovell, 1979; and—more sympathetically—O'Connell, 1982), the teaching procedures have also been enthusiastically received.

To some extent the responsibility for our viewing these three methods as similar must be the responsibility of Stevick (1976), who—after a brilliant exposition of the weaknesses of traditional, particularly audiolingually orientated methodology and of various investigations supporting the view that meaning could not be seen as peripheral to the language-learning/language-using process, described these three as examples for teachers anxious to move towards more meaningful teaching. As Stevick's subsequent books have shown (1980, 1982), his view of the language teaching profession is entirely compatible with that outlined here, whereby the teacher collects from any source ideas for procedures and practices which can be integrated into an individual methodology, adjustable to the needs of particular classes and students. But it is possible to misinterpret his interest in alternative methodologies, particularly if we are mistakenly searching for the 'one true teaching method', as a much more final statement than it is intended to be.

What we have to decide is whether the significance of these methodologies is simply part of the sociology of language teaching—a product of the American educational system, or of particular socio-economic demands for English language courses— and consequently of no major significance for other approaches, or whether they have something important to tell us about language learning itself. Certainly, they demonstrate by their success the richness and complexity of a process which we are always inclined to over-simplify, if only to 'understand' it ourselves. Certainly, also, they show by their variety of procedure and of justification for procedure, the truth that students will learn in many varied and different ways, and this may lead us to suspect that no one student learns for precisely the same reason that the justifier of any particular method puts forward. But these three methods do share two features which should be important for us. All three of them are concerned with getting through, or under, the defences of the learner, with recognizing that learning a language is not simply learning a body of material, to be done by hard work and application. And all three are concerned with respecting the totality of the learner: the learner contributes to the learning process and does so with all faculties intact, not by isolating some small part, a language-learning facet in the personality. Now it is true that all good teaching had always been concerned with minimizing the defensiveness of learners, and creating a secure environment in which risks can be taken without loss of face. And it is also true that the holistic approach has been recognized as necessary in language learning outside the humanistic movement— for example in Wilkins's arguments about analytic and synthetic syllabuses (Wilkins, 1976: 3). But language is often still too much concerned with an intellectually learned code, imposed from outside by a teacher or textbook, with content which is entirely unnegotiable because the interactional opportunities for negotiation are not provided by the methodology, and with relevance to the learner imposed also from outside (whether through a needs rather than a wants analysis or through an essentially trivial-minded concern for major social issues, superficially dealt with in terms imposed by the textbook writer). Several surveys (for example, Mitchell, Parkinson and Johnstone, 1981: 32) have shown how rarely students in conventional foreign language classes ever speak to each other at all—and it is difficult to see how without doing this they are ever to have experience of producing the target language in natural and self-investing circumstances. Nor does much foreign language teaching observe the precepts of Lozanov:

> The important thing is that these recordings are not the conventional type of exercise for the repetition of lessons and for memorizing lexical and grammatical elements. They must be whole meaningful texts (not of a fragmentary nature) and, above all, interesting. It is important that no analysis and no translation of all the different elements of these recordings are made. They must be listened to for the sake of the music of the foreign speech. The meaning of the speech should be left to surface in the minds of the students, by itself, without stress and without any unpleasant efforts.
>
> (Lozanov, 1978: 277)

But there are strong arguments in contemporary research in language acquisition, both with mother tongues and foreign languages (see Krashen, 1981, for example), for an approach like this.

One of the most interesting aspects of suggestopaedic technique, and one which might appear to conflict with the demand for genuine personal interaction in the other methods, is the insistence that learners adopt a persona that is not their own. Instead of the casual role-play of much other communicative teaching, learners are expected to 'become' a member of the target culture with a personality and history prescribed for them. This is an aspect which Leontiev (1981), in an interesting Soviet discussion of Suggestopaedia, explores in some detail. Not only does the role adopted afford psychological protection in the early stages of learning, but it also allows for the possibility of creativity which may be inhibited by the conventions linked with the learner's mother-tongue-associated self. This wholesale role-adoption has the merit of partially resolving one of the great paradoxes of communicative teaching. A classroom is by definition preparatory, and constrained in ways that real language activity is not constrained. By trying to be realistic through analysis of real-life needs and an emphasis on use of the language, the conventional communicative classroom simply draws attention to the disjuncture between the class and its purpose. Role-play places the game element central to the conception of the activity, but at a high enough level of generality for the total communicative system of the language to be operable. Thus learners do not have to be personally committed too heavily to the content, while at the same time having the opportunity to develop the linguistic system as an integrated, meaningful system. We do not need to claim that the procedure should be adopted wholesale to be willing to explore its significance in the context of conventional methodology. Certainly it provides a pedagogical device within which context rules, rather than code rules (to use Widdowson's distinction: 1979: 194) can be developed. It is important for our understanding of the significance of role, however, that we should investigate the relation between the adopted role and the learner's own personal contributions as linguistic capacities develop. This issue is touched on by Leontiev (1981: 121), but it requires much more monitoring before the exact effect of this pedagogic device can be assessed.

This issue provides one example suitable for piecemeal investigation and mainstream experimentation. There are many others within the methods under discussion, both more specific and more general than this one. But what we must resist is pressure to accept either the whole package or none of it. We can recognize that the various elements are often systematically related to each other within the package, and that the system will itself be of interest. But we need also to believe that there is no guru who is granted more than partial understanding, and that there is no teacher, researcher or learner who cannot potentially improve on earlier work. Our problems are never exactly their problems, and what use we make of other's work must not be constrained by anything other than the desire to solve our own problems most effectively.

In other words, there are arguments for interpreting methods for which success has been claimed as data to be accounted for in the framework of current theories the nature of language acquisition. But there is no compelling reason for thinking that a particular method is, or ever can be, a complete solution to language teaching problems. Only when people become predictable, and their communication and conceptualizing needs capable of being programmed, shall we expect there to be one true method of language learning. And if that time ever looks like coming, I hope that most of us will have left language teaching for some more subversive activity.

Caring and Sharing in the Foreign Language Class: a review of Gertrude Moskowitz

(a review from *English Language Teaching Journal*, October 1981.
An earlier version appeared in the *BAAL Newsletter*)

You're an intelligent person! I know you are, for you are reading *ELTJ*, and I want you to know that I know because I'm a humanistic teacher! You want to know why I'm writing like this? Well you certainly ask all the incisive questions! I need to write like this because I've got to give you some idea of the style of Gertrude Moskowitz's book. OK? Fine! Now we can start! I guess we really know each other now that we've built up a genuine relationship.

Or maybe not . . .

It would be unfair to imply that the whole of the book is written like this, but there is enough of it to be worrying. Because it is certainly catching! And basically deceitful! You agree with me? Of course you do, because no well-meaning person wouldn't, and I know you're a humanistic teacher or you wouldn't be reading this book. And I haven't given you any other option! I've won, you see.

Or did someone interrupt? If they did, I didn't hear.

*   *   *   *   *

There is a serious problem here with the conventions of written discourse. Normally the reader has some freedom of manoeuvre, and can blame the writer for failing to predict the questions which will be asked. But here the writer gives the reader all the responses. 'You've been an ideal listener and have asked a number of pertinent questions, which I hope I've answered' we are told on p.39. Professor Moskowitz's view of sympathy seems to include a confident anticipation of the reader's reactions, with the result that the reader's sympathy is not requested, but kidnapped and held hostage. Those who are resistant to affective interaction are made to feel in some way anti-humanistic. One feels that the book is constantly on its guard against the unspecified enemy: dry, academic, inhuman teachers peering and jeering at the foreign language classroom.

But we have to be very careful. Several ex-students of mine have remarked that this is one of the most helpful books they have read on classroom techniques, and certainly many of the exercises recommended will be both valuable and popular with classes. After about 40 pages of introductory discussion, there are 180 pages of actual classroom activities and materials, associated with comments on preparation, writing and training teachers. The emphasis is commendably practical, and no teacher or teacher trainer should disagree with the re-orientation towards the affective domain which is the main motivation for the book. Furthermore, Professor Moskowitz's credentials are impeccable. She has made lasting contributions to our understanding of interaction in the foreign language classroom, and is an admired and highly experienced teacher and teacher trainer. Anything she writes must deserve our attention.

Yet I am unwilling to concede that differing tastes or differing traditions are adequate explanations for my uncertainty. Partly, I feel that probing too readily into the personal feelings of the learner becomes impertinent. The teacher–student relationship is unavoidably asymmetrical. However kindly, well-meaning and democratic the teacher, the learner has less liberty to reject overtures than the teacher has, and the teacher should not presume upon the relationship: learners must be free to decide how deeply to participate. If 'whole-person' involvement is not treated sensitively and subtly it will become dangerously simplistic. Constantly keeping our feelings to ourselves is inhibiting rather than freeing (p.102) is a maxim to be examined and perhaps approved by psychiatrists, but it is unhelpful, even dangerous, as advice to someone ignorant of the uses and abuses of psychiatry. And anyway, how genuine can the response be to (for example) exercise 49 (p.114) which has as one of its aims 'to give students the opportunity to express warm thoughts and feelings'? Each member of the class has to tell the class something performed by one of the other students which they particularly liked, enjoyed or appreciated. As an exercise, this may produce reasonably contextualized language, but to what extent can genuinely 'positive' thoughts be produced to order? How do such exercises really relate to the 'shift in society's focus' towards 'developing fulfilling relationships, recognizing interdependence, expressing one's feelings, achieving one's potential, sharing oneself' referred to in the initial justification of the approach, on page 10? Are not human beings a little more complicated than all this implies?

The book is decorated with 'humanistic posters' based on slogans from a variety of sources. 'If you want to be loved, then love' (p.218). 'The rainbow is prettier than the pot of gold at the end because the rainbow is *now*' (p.233). Is it a trivial point that such cracker-mottoes obscure more than they reveal: how much great literature could survive the former, and how is education compatible with the latter?

Many of the ideas for classroom activities are worth adapting and adopting, but I am constantly being reminded of a film I once saw of a mime about Vietnam performed by a boy's club. After some skilful but stereotyped portrayals of the Americans, Vietcong and villagers, lasting about fifteen minutes, the presenter of the film turned to his audience. 'Now', he exclaimed, 'now these boys really *understand* about Vietnam.' We all want to care and share, and this book does show us many useful ways of doing the latter. But can we truly *care* by oversimplifying so grossly? I wonder.

Graded Material and the Use of the Lexicon

(review of Roland Hindmarsh, *Cambridge English Lexicon*, 1980.
From *BAAL Newsletter* **11**, Marsh 1981)

The 1970s have been the years of discourse and interlanguage, of ESP, functions and notions, so when a two hundred page word list arrives in the post, the result of more than ten years' work, initial reaction may well be surprise—even shock. Surely the time for pedagogical word lists is past, if we still need to consult them why cannot we simply use a modified Michael West, are we not concerned with texts rather than words, with authentic reading rather than isolated items, with the needs of individual students rather than linguistic generalizations, however precise? Anyway, is not the whole notion of simplification under fire? Two years ago an acute reviewer in *ARELS Journal* remarked of simplified readers:

> People who write foreign language readers are a strange, almost unique, species of writer: they set out to write something (but it doesn't really matter what) for a totally unknown sector of the public (age, nationality, background, mentality, interests, all unknown) in a painfully emasculated form of their language . . . There is a vast market for their work and yet there are not many that can withstand the close scrutiny of the native speaker. (M. Lesley Gore, *ARELS Journal*, Vol.2, No.10, 1978: 255)

It has been argued that graded readers establish an allegedly scientific series of steps which then have to be correlated with the quite unmeasurable levels of students—unmeasurable because of the difficulty of trading off against each other such disparate factors as personal interest, linguistic level, intellectual and cultural sophistication, imaginative capacity and simple time available. A correlation of the precise with the imprecise is not worth attempting. And, of course, most of us have our favourite horror stories of publishers' editors rejecting anything interesting in favour of anything dull ('she was coming to the evening of her life' becomes 'she was very ill') on the assumption that learners of English come to reading as blank and unliterary and inhuman as the computers on which the prevalent information transfer metaphor is based.

All in all, many of us will be predisposed to react negatively to even the idea let alone the solid fact of another pedagogic lexicon, however up-to-date and rigorous its basis. But perhaps one indication of its relevance can be tested by seeing the extent to which the compiler is himself aware of the doubts his work may engender and the misuses to which it may be put. Roland Hindmarsh's introduction discusses his own personal interest in grading and wordlists, and outlines the genesis of this one. He rightly comments that in the 1960s vocabulary grading, and later syntactic grading, were enormously influential in ESL publishing, but then goes on to refer briefly to the implications of a sociolinguistic approach to language. 'Purpose, context, tone, mode and medium can be orchestrated to produce a language specification: but that specification can—and I maintain must—be graded in some measure to make it right for where the learner is now' (p.vi). This sounds a strong statement, but it is modified almost immediately: instruments of language selection 'cannot be allowed to dominate syllabus ever again; they are however needed to ensure good husbandry in learning to use language in specific situations'. And again, instruments for the grading of vocabulary, syntax and discourse (the last 'as yet unwritten') 'must be used flexibly in the generation of language learning programmes; but that they are an essential part of this process there can be no doubt'. Flexible use is illustrated also: 'for some users this may mean no more than an occasional check on vocabulary items; for others a filter at a particular stage in the production of language learning materials; for yet others, a careful scrutiny to establish that a reading comprehension passage for an examination does not contain vocabulary items that exceed a given learning level by more than the agreed degree of variation'.

So the author is aware of the problems. How useful is the list, as presented, in helping us to solve them? There seem to be three important issues here: first, how reliable is the list as a representative and principled selection? second, how accessible is the material if we do want to consult it? and third, what advice is given us about the significance of the information we can obtain from it?

On the issue of reliability, it is difficult to give a satisfactory answer without extensive experience of using it. The principles of selection, as outlined, are unhelpful here. Michael West's 'General Service List' (Longman, 1953) has been extended and modified by comparison with a number of other lists, including Thorndike and Lorge, Kucera and Francis, Wright and a variety of others (conveniently summarized on pp.x-xi). But the account of the process of selection refers to a number of unspecified selection procedures. Some items 'did not meet certain criteria of statistical constancy', others were 'slightly archaic', 'academic' or 'specialized' in spite of being of high frequency in other word counts. Other criteria used include 'intuitions of teachers of EFL' and 'lexical items reflecting the world today . . . drawn together from a number of sources'. Consequently we cannot claim that this list represents more than one person's (though with considerable consultation) subjective opinion of the most useful selection; though we must concede that the subjective opinion has been cross-referenced with the standard sources, and based on an extensive and varied experience in teaching English overseas. Yet none of this need detract from the merit of the book. If Hindmarsh has good intuitions, this half-scientific, half-intuitive procedure may take us closer to what actually works than something more objective. The material has already been used as a basis for the Cambridge English Language Learning readers, one of the more successful reading schemes, and it has been related to the comprehension range necessary for passing Cambridge First Certificate. But in the last resort, we must depend on experience. The question of reliability, if the compiler defends intuitive procedures, can only be answered in terms of eventual usefulness, and we should ask the question again in five years' time. At this stage, we can only report that the manner of compilation makes sense, given the premises on which it is based, and a superficial survey of the contents does not reveal any striking anomalies.

On accessibility, this lexicon can be recommended. About 4500 lexical items are included in the main list, and each is graded on a five-point scale, five being approximately Cambridge First Certificate level. It is claimed, but only experience will enable us to tell, that the five levels can be linked neatly with the five levels in Longman's 'English Grammatical Structure' (Alexander *et al.*, 1975). The number of words in each level, going upwards, are: 598, 517, 992, 1034 and 1229. The 4500 words are accompanied by a breakdown of semantic values, each value being graded on the same scale, except that these values extend up to levels six and seven, the last being provisionally the level required for the Cambridge Certificate of Proficiency. The inclusion of semantic values takes the number of distinguishable meanings up to about 8000, and in addition a large number of appendices give proper names, phrasal verbs and a range of semantic and morphological problem areas specific treatment within the same scale of grading. By and large the information is more easily retrievable than in other comparable reference works.

As was suggested in the discussion of reliability, it is difficult to evaluate the compilation procedures. Consequently, it is difficult to establish the significance of the information gained from the lexicon, except for taking on trust that it has worked for materials writers in the past. For this reason, it would have been helpful to have been given some information about how it has been used, and, particularly, how flexible writers found themselves being, what criteria for exceptions were established in the process of making simplifications of texts, and what other difficulties they encountered. It might have been particularly helpful if the following rules of thumb had been suggested:

1. Clarify in your own mind the type of learner you are writing for, as precisely as possible.
2. Write your text as clearly and appropriately as you can, without any reference to the lexicon.
3. Check it, with the help of at least one other competent person, and consult the lexicon for all lexical items in problem areas, regardless of how certain you are of their suitability.
4. Wherever the lexicon conflicts with your text examine the context for support, perhaps interpolate paraphrase or explanation if that can be done easily, and only change the item if that can be done without effort.
5. Never let the lexicon outweigh your own convictions, but do let it inform and sensitize your judgement.

In a nutshell, the lexicon should be used negatively by writers, not positively. Only in this way will the writing of materials remain writing. As Michael West has remarked, 'those most likely to do this work effectively would themselves be capable of selling an original story or novel' (West, 1964). A couple of pages of discussion along these lines would improve the lexicon greatly, and prevent its being used as a straight-jacket on interesting writing. Hindmarsh several times indicates that word levels are not everything without giving even the most intuitive help about how to limit their potential stranglehold. As Humpty Dumpty reminds Alice, 'The question is, which is to be master. That's all.' (Carroll, 1872).

This last point is really an important one. A word list such as this one does provide us with a common point of reference, and such a point of reference enables writers to defend themselves against insensitive editors. But it risks making the limited aspects of language which are at the moment susceptible to clear, even if intuitive classification the dominant ones in materials writing. However scientifically-based the materials, they must stand or fall on whether they relate genuinely to the reader. Colour and humour may be far more important than word level, information control may prevent readers from doing what all native-speaking readers do—allow approximate meanings (Ripon is a place in Britain, it does not matter for the purposes of the story whereabouts), and much EFL publishing policy may lead to the conclusion that foreign readers are ignorant, stupid and illiterate in their mother tongues. Readers for EFL/ESL need redundancy, need interest, need to be more difficult than learners can cope with linguistically, but not too much more, and above all need to be written by people who can write well. Otherwise they are likely to train foreign learners in how *not* to read. The Cambridge English Lexicon is to be welcomed as a potentially most useful weapon. But we must be careful who we point it at.

Note: I have discussed a number of points made in this review with various colleagues, to whom I am most grateful, particularly Monica Vincent.

Seven Last Slogans

(from *Modern English Teacher*, **7**, 1, September 1979)

These are tough times for EFL methodologists: the thought was drummed into me as I sat in my car in a snow drift last spring, with a blizzard driving snow into the engine and the news from Iran coming over the radio. I was returning from an RSA lecture, and it occurred to me—as it has on several occasions before when I have narrowly missed revolutions, hijacks or wars—that there are things I want to say to the EFL world rather urgently. I failed to write the messages in a bottle, to be dug up with my frozen body; instead, I propose—not for the first time—to use *MET* as a bottle substitute.

All of which is to say that, if I wait till I have written an article on each of the topics touched on here, I shall still be waiting when the bullet does catch me, so I have compiled a short list of slogans which I feel to be too widely believed in the EFL world, and added brief notes about why they should be rejected. The mode is arrogant, but the intention is to stimulate discussion. I am sure that, in their various ways, all these issues do need to be discussed.

So—dogmatically—here are some of your beliefs, implicit if not explicit; please question them.

To teachers and teacher trainers:
EXCITING TECHNIQUES MAKE GOOD TEACHING

We don't know what makes good teaching, though we can be sure that some things make bad teaching. Exciting techniques excite teachers, and their excitement may communicate itself to students, but learning needs to be calm, slow and steady at times. Above all, too much concentration on vigorous skills distracts from the duller but more important matter of working to a steadily developing scheme which is systematically planned. It is true that we often need to perform in the classroom, but education is not the same as performance; education is about development, and that can only take place over a period. Teachers must concentrate on organizing work over a long period.

To teachers, writers and publishers:
TEXTBOOKS HELP TEACHERS

They can, but many of them don't. There is no *Which* for textbooks, and masses of rubbish is skilfully marketed. Even the best textbooks take away initiative from teachers by implying that there is somewhere an 'expert' who can solve problems for your students and your class. We need resource packs, sets of materials with advice to teachers on how to adapt and modify the contents. Such materials do exist, but—for good commercial reasons—publishers will still seek the money-making coursebook. Educational and commercial criteria are here directly in conflict, for global textbooks prevent local initiative by providing a sense of false security: experts can only advise, they cannot substitute for local responsibility.

To writers and publishers:

THE TESTING OF PUBLISHED MATERIALS CAN BE LEFT TO THE OPEN MARKET; IT IS NOT THE RESPONSIBILITY OF THE PUBLISHER OR AUTHOR

More than one big name in the business has told me that he simply types and sends to his publisher. Surely, to put a book on the open market implies a moral contract that that book has been cleared of basic faults. Clearly, methods cannot be easily evaluated, but books could have basic procedural faults eliminated by trial in one or two classes. Why can there not be a publishers' agreement that no manuscript will be looked at without a detailed description being provided of class trial and an indication of the modifications which have been made as a result of such trial? Many—perhaps most—teaching materials show clearly that they have scarcely been near a classroom in their published form: any teacher can give many examples. To publish manifestly unusable materials (however interesting the ideas) is to steal from the buyer.

To publishers:

A 'SCIENTIFIC' GRADING OF READING MATERIALS IS NOT ONLY POSSIBLE, BUT USEFUL

We certainly need an approximate *ordering* of reading materials for particular students, matched against a generalized ordering of student progress. But, however effectively we can measure reading matter, we cannot measure the students against which it is to be matched. And anyway, students do not read—thank goodness— material which is appropriate linguistically, but materials which they are interested in, and each student differs in his interests. Much more effort should be devoted to reporting on books which have been enjoyed by particular types of student, and thus establishing an ordering of appropriate reading matter. What evidence is there at all to relate the ordering established, admittedly quite rigorously, by linguists, to the ordering of *content* demanded by students who want the opportunity to read fluently?

To trainers of EFL teachers:

EFL TEACHING NEEDS MORE SPECIALIZATION

EFL teaching is a volatile profession, and its practitioners will always be liable to move from country to country and from teaching situation to teaching situation. This can be an advantage as well as a disadvantage, for it prevents stagnation. But we need teachers who can adapt as times and places change, and we need experts whose expertise is based on direct practical experience. There are already too many people designing syllabuses, writing materials and advising with too little acquaintance with straightforward classroom teaching. Specialists will of course need training, but this should come later after plenty of general experience. There are many essential teaching abilities which can *only* be acquired by many years' full-time class teaching. Specialists without these abilities are top heavy and should be pushed over.

To teacher trainers and administrators:

EFL TEACHING AND THE BRITISH EDUCATIONAL SYSTEM CANNOT COMBINE

It used to be fashionable to postulate a great divide between EFL and ESL. In fact, if you look closely at—say—Sweden, Malta, Kenya, Romania, the Netherlands, and second language work in the States and Britain, it is clear that there is a very confused picture indeed, and certainly no obvious two categories. Understanding social, psychological, political and other dimensions of language teaching will require similar training for all these situations, and techniques appropriate for any of them may have relevance for some students in any other. Teachers who have taught overseas, particularly in India or Pakistan and the West Indies, have something to offer in the British state sector which no one who has not spent a long period in such countries can provide. Any teacher who has taught overseas can offer experience of living in a foreign culture which should be able to be utilized in multi-cultural British schools. PGCE trained EFL/ESL students, particularly, are grossly under-used in British education: they do not offer the same as students trained in other subjects, but they can offer some things which nobody else can, and they could have a role to play, not only in specific ESL units, but in mother tongue and foreign language departments also. No other type of teacher, in general, can offer as close involvement with language problems in multi-cultural settings, both through training and experience. A career-structure incorporating much greater opportunities for interchange between overseas and home teaching is needed, and local authorities need to be far more aware than they are of what they can gain by recruiting teachers with appropriate EFL experience.

To everyone:

COPYRIGHT LAWS NEED TO BE STRENGTHENED AGAINST NON-COMMERCIAL USES

The copyright laws are anti-educational, particularly those relating to off-air copying of radio and television. (They may also be incorrect economically, as the more people exposed to—say—Larkin's poems at school, the more people likely to buy his and others' poetry in later life.) Certainly, quotation within reason by educational institutions should be legalized. Surely it is not too difficult to charge a general copyright fee on all duplicating and copyrighting apparatus, and waive the specific fees for education. Ideas and art should be acknowledged, but they are not to be owned as property: they belong to us all.

I thank you for your indulgence. Now, with a clear conscience, I can be released to that special purgatory reserved for EFL teachers. You will recall that, in *A Handful of Dust*, Tony Last is left for ever reading the works of Dickens to the mad Mr Todd. How much more preferable that is to the EFL limbo, for ever teaching to unreceptive students the collected textbooks of Mr ******. But this name is copyright!

Section Four:

TOWARDS A METHODOLOGY FOR LITERATURE TEACHING

The three papers in this section follow on the one in *Problems and Principles in English Teaching* about the Tanzanian experience (Brumfit, 1970). They are attempting to develop basic principles for the discussion of methodology in the teaching of literature. Language teaching has for many years been able to draw upon sophisticated discussion of teaching methodology, but literature teaching has rarely been self-conscious about criteria for syllabus organization or for teaching methods, and when it has addressed these questions it has usually been moving away from the model of literature teaching assumed here.

These papers all assume that the reason for teaching literature, ultimately, is so that as many people as possible will read and enjoy great works of international literature. The path to this goal may be indirect, but there is an assumption that not to have access to, for example, *War and Peace* or *Waiting for Godot* or Wordsworth's poetry is to be deprived of a valuable educational and human experience for anyone who is brought up within the western educational tradition. Appreciation of masterpieces does not prevent us from recognizing that 'being a masterpiece' may be subject to fashion, and that the concept of 'a masterpiece' is problematic. But as long as critics and readers like to share serious works to facilitate exchange of ideas, and as long as there is some agreement over which are the most interesting works to think about, the concept of a highly-valued text as a masterpiece will have some use. What is important educationally is the attested quality of the experience of reading certain works for many critics and teachers. To be wide-ranging and eclectic in taste is not to deny the notion of taste altogether, and I do not subscribe to the view that all reading can be equally valuable (nor to the view that reading is a unique path to virtue, I should add). For those with an interest in reading, teaching should help by steering a path towards the best (i.e. the least simplified and the most truthful) accounts of the human predicament. Ideas in this section are developed more fully in *Literature and Language Teaching*, edited by C. J. Brumfit and R. A. Carter, forthcoming from Oxford University Press in 1985.

Reading Skills and the Study of Literature in a Foreign Language

(from *System* **9**, 1, 1981)

This paper is a preliminary attempt to consider the relationship between reading in a foreign language and the teaching of literature. It is preliminary because this is an area which has been neglected in recent discussions of language teaching, while practice has continued to relate the two. Because this is a question which has been little discussed in relation to current language teaching theory, this paper will be essentially philosophical and discursive in approach. It will also attempt a consideration of approaches to literature in principle, reduced to basic categories which may be helpful to teachers, in order to set in context the difficulties of teachers of literature in foreign languages.

The problem

Recent approaches to language teaching (outlined, for example, in Widdowson, 1978; Brumfit and Johnson, 1979) have ignored literature teaching. However, increasing recognition of the difficulties of communicative syllabuses (see contributors to Johnson and Morrow, 1978; and Muller, 1980) have led to a more cautious approach. It is not necessary to retreat, though, to turn again with interest to literature teaching, for literature provides us with a convenient source of content for a course in a foreign language, and a truly notional syllabus will need to be constructed round concepts and subject matter which develop in complexity (Widdowson and Brumfit, 1981). Most attempts to provide motivating and communicative material for learners are strong in technique but weak in any sense of developmental structure (Moskowitz, 1978; Maley and Duff, 1978; Melville *et al.*, 1980). Even courses intended for school use (Abbs and Sexton, 1978; Jupp *et al.*, 1979) suffer from fragmentation of content.

This paper is not an attempt to argue that literature teaching ought to be used to solve these problems. It does set out to argue the role that literature teaching might have at fairly advanced levels. A clarification of this may have implications for what could happen during more elementary teaching, and is worth doing for several reasons. First, reading is the most autonomous and individualizable ability in language work, and literature is a rich and widely-appealing source of material for reading. Second, literature is one of only three areas on which a foreign language *content* syllabus could be based (the others are linguistics and civilization) which will not conflict with the claims of other subjects in the curriculum. Third, materials are readily available. But all of these reasons are subservient to the argument that there must be a content which is in itself worthwhile if advanced language teaching is to be really effective. This is not simply a matter of motivation, but of the nature of language: functional and notional development requires some basis in a developing body of information, procedures and skills to be exploited in the target language.

Literary competence

Culler writes (1975: 114):

> '. . . anyone wholly unacquainted with literature and unfamiliar with the conventions by which fictions are read, would . . . be quite baffled if presented with a poem. His knowledge of the language would enable him to understand phrases and sentences, but he would not know, quite literally, what to *make* of this strange concatenation of phrases. He would be unable to read it *as* literature . . . because he lacks the complex 'literary competence' which enables others to proceed. He has not internalized the 'grammar' of literature which would permit him to convert linguistic sequences into literary structures and meanings.'

A true literature syllabus will not be simply the use of literary texts for advanced language purposes, but an attempt to develop or extend literary competence. But to do this involves clarifying a concept which is still contentious in terms which are simple enough to be related to classroom practice for inexperienced readers.

While it is true that there can be no final reading of a literary text—the meaning is always subject to negotiation for it results from the relationship between reader(s) and writer—it is nonetheless possible to make an inappropriate response through a misunderstanding of the codes being operated. Such codes will be not solely linguistic, but will include the interplay of event with event, relationships between characters, exploitation of ideas and value systems, formal structure in terms of a genre or other literary convention, and relationships between any of these and the world outside literature itself. All of these, and other aspects too, will be subject to convention, and writers will exploit the conventions they inherit in different ways. A good reader recognizes such conventions (though not necessarily explicitly) and interprets them in relation to the world of other experience which literature must in some sense imitate or comment on.

The codes cited above—and they do not of course, constitute a definitive list—vary in complexity and accessibility. Most works of literature are accessible in terms of plot (events) and relationships between characters, though the fact of such accessibility will lead some writers to insist on falsifying our expectations and deliberately operating with ambiguity and confusion. But certain kinds of interaction, for example with political ideas, will demand sophistication of response in terms of outside understanding of, for example, political theories. Such considerations will force us to consider literature not as an isolated activity but as one to be viewed in relation to the general cognitive development of the student. There has been some work in this direction, but there is much still to be done in clarifying the situation, even with mother tongue readers (Whitehead *et al.*, 1977; Blunt, 1977; Thomson, 1979).

Relations with pedagogy

It should be clear from this discussion so far that the teaching of literature cannot simply involve an extension of ordinary reading skills. It is possible to be a competent reader and unfamiliar with literary conventions associated with a particular culture. Nonetheless, language use requires recognition of the density of allusion that humanity is capable of and that any language exploits. All users of language share this common basis and it is from this that a specifically literary education must develop. So for a literary pedagogy to be successful the teaching must develop the literary awareness which is implicit in learners' ability to use language at all, and sensitize learners to the conventions of the literary tradition. To attempt this in a foreign language is a demanding task, made more difficult by the confusion which reigns in the teaching of mother tongue literature.

The teaching of literature in a foreign language must still be partially dependent on approaches taken to teaching mother tongue literature, so some attempt to clarify this neglected area is necessary (for some indication of the range of approaches available see Brinke, 1977: 175ff; Marshall, 1972: 29ff).

Ideally, a literature syllabus in the mother tongue will not only exploit understanding of language, but will relate to other aesthetic work, art and music, for example. It must, that is to say, be responsive to the total educational and cultural context, so that the form it takes will vary from situation to situation. Sometimes, indeed, for example in some Third World countries, foreign language literatures will take upon themselves the major part of literary education, and will need to be related to traditions of oral literature, and the relation of contemporary indigenous literature with the ex-colonial cultures. Here, it will be difficult to avoid major political issues since linguistic and cultural relations will be so bound up with issues of power and development (Brumfit, 1970; Pettit, 1971; Searle, 1972). In the traditional foreign language teaching contexts of European countries the differences between various local mother tongue traditions will be crucial elements in relating to the world literary tradition. But it should be possible to specify usefully, though in general terms, the basic needs of learners of literary competence.

Relationship with advanced reading

This paper makes no claim that the reading of literature requires different reading strategies from other kinds of reading. It does make a claim, though, that reading which exploits literary perceptions will require a different pedagogical approach. Responding to literature is not a matter of basic understanding of the language of the text. It is the significance of the text that is important to the good reader, not its ability to be translated exactly. Most native speaking readers of (say) Shakespeare will fail to understand a proportion, even at the literal level, of what they read or hear, but this failure will not be crucial to their response unless it develops above a certain level. Accepting appropriate tolerance of uncertainty is an essential part of being a good reader. Consequently, work in literature follows naturally from integrative activities in reading, in which understanding of the text is derived from discussion by students of questions which force them to see the text as a coherent piece of discourse (see, for example, Munby, 1968). Reading strategies which make use of explicit analytical devices will have less relevance.

A simple pedagogical model for literature teaching

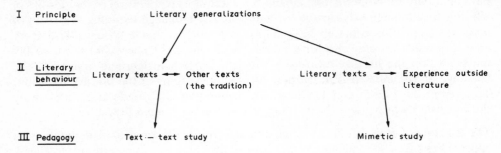

I   Principle   Literary generalizations

II   Literary
     behaviour   Literary texts ←→ Other texts   Literary texts ←→ Experience outside
                                   (the tradition)   literature

III Pedagogy   Text — text study   Mimetic study

The argument to justify a simple model of this kind is as follows:

1. The teaching of appropriate reading of literature cannot proceed primarily by linear means, for insofar as it is a mature reading process response to the text in all its aspects must develop simultaneously.
2. The fundamental ability of a good reader of literature is the ability to generalize from the given text to either other aspects of the literary tradition or personal or social significances outside literature.
3. These two fields of reference outside any particular text must be developed by any effective teaching theory, and techniques in literature teaching are only worthwhile insofar as they serve these two aims.
4. Students must be assisted to develop their latent abilities in both these directions, and this implies establishing criteria for grading their exposure to literature in terms of these.
5. The prime purpose of any specifically literary work in school is not to provide particular items of knowledge, but to use such knowledge as tokens in the process of generalization referred to in (2) above.
6. (a) The ability to perceive and explore relationships between literary texts and other literary texts (hence developing understanding of the notion of convention and tradition) will be developed by reading texts deliberately associated with each other for pedagogical purposes. Texts may be linked by subject matter, by formal and structural similarity, by thematic intention, or by any other appropriate device.

   (b) The ability to perceive and explore relationships between literary texts and ordinary life will be developed through increasing familiarity with the various mimetic properties of literature. Pedagogically, this is best achieved by grading the complexity and subtlety of external reference in the texts used, for example by starting with relatively simple allegorical and mythical works from which generalizing to personal or external experience can be made as simple as possible.

Implications of such a model for foreign language work

Work on foreign language literatures must be consistent with the position outlined above, but students will be able to work at varying levels of sophistication, according to their previous experience of literature: their literary understanding will not correlate with their linguistic. Hence criteria for the selection of teaching materials will have to anticipate a disjuncture between linguistic and literary form. Language level alone is not an appropriate criterion. And furthermore, the work in the foreign language, if it is to be truly literary work, must be regarded as an extension of capacities already developed, at least partially, in mother tongue literary work, but these capacities will be refined through contact with literature from a foreign culture.

Stating the arguments thus starkly runs the risk of appearing both pretentious and simplistic, but it is worth trying to be over-simple in this particular discussion, for tradition is strong and needs to be assaulted by relatively clear and unrefined arguments. It needs to be argued forcefully that literature teaching is about abilities, not knowledge, and that these abilities are totally bound up with the network of conventions which all writers choose to exploit. Foreign language literature teaching must respond to this as much as mother tongue literature teaching.

However, once an argument along these lines is accepted, it is possible to list the basic criteria for the selection of texts for advanced work in teaching foreign literatures. (The examples given are drawn from English literature, but the principles would apply to any.)

First, a group of criteria which relate to reading of any kind:

1. *Linguistic level.* This can of course be measured in lexical or syntactic terms. But it is essential to recognize that no descriptive linguistic model can measure significance in literary terms. Blake's poems, or Hemingway's *The Old Man and the Sea*, are examples of linguistically simple texts which pose considerable problems in literary terms.
2. *Cultural level.* Different works of literature will be close to the cultural and social expectations of different groups of learners. This may affect decisions in various ways. For example, nineteenth-century literary modes are culturally closer to the reading experience of relatively unsophisticated readers than many contemporary works. In some Third World countries eighteenth-century works such as Fielding or Crabbe may strike immediate chords because local society is still (just) pre-industrial.
3. *Length.* Still a crucial pedagogical factor.

Such criteria may be applied, with appropriate modification, to any reading materials, but there are three others which are significant in purely literary terms:

4. *Pedagogical role* (in relation to the literature-literature or literature-life connections). At appropriate levels works which are satisfactory on other grounds may be linked to others (Golding's *Lord of the Flies* linked to Ballantyne's *The Coral Island* on which it is a deliberate comment, for example, or linked to other books on a similar theme, such as Susan Hill's *I'm the King of the Castle*). Or books may be deliberately read in connection with contemporary events (novels of Graham Greene, perhaps).
5. *Genre representation.* If the course is truly concerned with developing reading

capacities, it cannot be restricted to short stories and poems which can be studied in class. All normal types of literature need to be available.

6. *Classic status* (or 'face validity'). Some texts may be demanded and therefore motivating for students, even though they are not essential on other grounds. The desire to read Dickens or Shakespeare may enable students to overcome difficulties which would be significant in terms of the other criteria.

Conclusion

The development of literary abilities in the way outlined here presupposes a fairly fluent capacity to read English. But the grading of literature teaching texts and strategies will have to take into account a great deal more than simple knowledge of the language. What literature teaching can offer, though, is a basis for a truly notional development of a language syllabus. The criteria for selection and use of literary texts, played off against each other, must lead to a recognition of the needs of particular groups of students. Students' authentic responses to the literary tradition will both assist the development of appropriate syllabuses, through trial and error, and will be developed through a carefully graded sequence of texts. If reading is to be viewed as an integrated process, the teaching of reading must do more than simply exercise reading in the target language. Literary texts, if used in relation to a serious view of extending literary competence, will provide a particularly suitable base from which motivated language activity can develop. In this paper, necessarily somewhat condensed, it has been possible to give only the barest outline of a new approach. But this seems to be a direction worth exploring in further work.

Wider Reading for Better Reading: an alternative approach to teaching literature

(from *The School Librarian*, **27**, 1, March 1979)

This article describes an attempt to reject the 'set books' approach to teaching literature at sixth-form level and above, and instead to develop with students an attitude to works of literature which should lead to a mature approach to their subsequent reading. Most people seem to agree that the set books at A level should be supported by the reading of a wide range of other works, but very few schools can honestly claim to establish the habit of wide, serious reading in their students. Perhaps one reason for our failure is that we do not actually ask students in schools and colleges to read in the same ways as we would expect to read ourselves. The course which is described below tries to help students to discuss books in relation to their experience of other books within similar traditions, as well as in relation to knowledge and experience gained outside literature altogether. Inevitably, the young reader's experience, both of literature and life, is limited; but this is no reason to claim that books can be discussed only in relative isolation. We have to acquire the ability, which all good readers use as they read, to compare constantly, and there is no reason why the shape of the course should not help students to do this. Certainly if this does not happen there is a grave risk that connections and comparisons will always be those handed down by the teacher or at best drawn from secondary sources. Somehow we need to give students with a particular interest in literature the experience of reading and discovering not isolated texts but a whole body of literature—and of discussing this in relation to their experience both inside and outside literature. Perhaps it is hardly surprising that few adults read literature seriously after leaving school when the model placed before them has often been exclusively one of *study* of individual texts more or less in isolation.

The reading experience

For many of us, the profound pleasure of reading comes partly from an experience which is simultaneously individual and communal. We read alone for much of the time, but we share the experience not only of the writers but also of other readers with whom we can discuss our reading. And we do not usually discuss isolated books, and rarely passages of books. We discuss authors against other authors, genres, national traditions and whole epochs. Our response to literature is part of our response to history, to ethics, to politics, to understanding what we are and what other people are. In other words, we do not *have* knowledge of books, we *use* our knowledge: our response is both active and shared.

Four basic book lists

Students embarking on our course, then, were asked to read widely, to respond not to texts but to groups of texts, and to work together within a broad and flexible framework. We decided not to think in terms of set texts but of set fields, and produced four basic lists of books for students to opt for. (One of these lists can be found on p.114.) Four different criteria were used for the list selections: one taking a period—post-1945 English literature; one a genre—satire; one a theme—war literature; and one a national comparison (with a necessary time limitation)—twentieth-century American and Russian literature. Students chose to work successively on two of these fields, making their choice after looking at specimen lists of about twenty books within the general area specified by the title of the course. It was emphasized, however, that the fields were to be interpreted generously: students were completely at liberty to read and discuss any other appropriate books, and tutors expected to learn from what students read. It was not to be solely a one-way process.

The work programme

A student received the basic book list as long as possible before the beginning of term and read around the general area in any way that seemed appropriate. Contact hours could be used very flexibly by the tutor on each of the four courses. Usually, students themselves determined what would happen in the weeks ahead, with the main options available being:

(a) student-led seminars (led initially by groups of students, but later by individuals);
(b) tutor-led seminars (increasingly on topics requested by students);
(c) various forms of project, with small groups of students working with the tutor at any one time;
(d) one-to-one discussions with students.

Certain minimum requirements were laid down. Students were expected to read as many as possible of the books on the list, but the (very modest) official minimum was put at seven for each course. They were, however, expected to keep a reading record, in the form of notes on every book they read. Such notes could be on books of their own choosing, and plot retelling was not expected, though some students did prefer to make a fairly detailed record, for reference purposes. The record was to be more in the form of a reading diary, in which comments and opinions could be entered. However, the fact that it was to be looked at by tutors inevitably turned this into something of a chore, even though we did accept that some books would be non-starters for some students. It was quite legitimate to record that a book had been tried and given up, or had only been skimmed.

Written work

The other two pieces of written work demanded during each course were treated much more enthusiastically by students. The major piece of work was a long essay on a topic chosen by the student: and the shorter one was either a piece of practical analysis of a particular passage in a book, or a piece of original creative work associated with the field of the reading list.

A great deal of emphasis was given to the student's own choice of essay topic. The thought and discussion that gradually pinned down the topic, and the discipline that lay in the moulding of a precise wording both proved to be an excellent preparation for writing. Topics were also discussed publicly in seminars, if students wished, so that the problems of writing were integrated with the general reading discussions involving us all. Such discussions were particularly valuable when we were choosing appropriate topics for the shorter piece of work. Some fields lent themselves more obviously to creative work than others. It was difficult, for example, to write creatively within Russian and American literature, but imitation chapters of books read—serious parodies—were accepted, as were annotated anthologies of poems. In all options tape-recorded programmes, carefully scripted and with musical or other sound effects, could be submitted. Some students preferred to offer an intensive study of a short passage. This might take the form of a detailed examination of a particular short text, or alternatively it might involve selecting a particularly significant passage in a novel or other long work, and examining in detail its role in the structure of the whole work. Here, as with the essays, the process of selection was itself educational.

Although the emphasis was placed on direct work with the texts, students were not of course discouraged from gathering further relevant information. One group indeed compiled an enormous dossier of useful background information for their option, consisting of lists of relevant background books available in local libraries, lists of dates of publication of significant works of literature going well beyond the original list, brief biographical details of major authors, and a time-chart of world events which impinged on the authors of the works being read. Students made all the arrangements for the collection, writing up and production of this material. While there is a risk of such information becoming more important than the reading itself, it is easy for a tutor to step in gently if this appears to be happening, and such background information may often be a stimulus to further reading.

Teaching procedures

Students spent their time, then, reading the texts, writing comments in their reading record files, preparing for the formal assignments, gathering background information, preparing for seminar presentations, or doing anything else appropriate. Those who were happiest working alone could do so, but those who responded to group activities were able to work co-operatively also. Formal seminars sometimes discussed single books—which everyone had agreed to read in time—in considerable detail; sometimes they looked at several books by one author; and sometimes they looked at several different treatments of similar themes. Tutors produced occasional lectures, but only when requested to do so by students. Other formal activities included prepared play-readings, discussion of recordings of drama and poetry, and occasions when students and tutor all arrived with short poems or prose pieces to read and discuss.

To a considerable extent the students determined the teaching procedures and the books chosen, both those read personally and those discussed publicly. The option choices provide a common frame of reference which makes useful co-operative activity possible within the group, but within these limits each student is able to move relatively freely. Some students tend towards a more sociological and some to a more aesthetic approach. At this stage which direction they move in surely matters less than that they should develop confidence in the relevance of literature to their own development and in their ability to respond seriously with enough literary experience to be able to make a relatively informed response. At the same time, however, the close liaison between tutor and student (coupled, it should be said, with a considerable degree of staff-student rapport which developed in all groups) makes it possible for a detailed examination of critical premises to take place over the year. Such strands can be taken up in later work on a formal basis.

Conclusions

It is not being claimed here that any one of the ideas described is particularly original. The great value of the course lay in establishing what might be called a 'reading community': a group of people with varying experience of life and literature, and with the agreed aim of sharing their reading in both formal and informal situations. The ability to sustain such a feeling of community is partly a responsibility of the tutor; but all the tutors on this course felt they gained more by this procedure than they had by more traditional approaches. Students become extremely supportive when there is a structure strong enough to appear authoritative but not strong enough to be authoritarian. In our reading communities we were all engaged on the same task: trying to increase our understanding of some aspect of literature. Tutors were not so much teaching, as setting up the conditions for learning and facilitating the process as it happened. We had not necessarily read all the books which students produced, but this did not matter, for we were concerned with a relationship to books, not with knowledge about a particular set of works. Knowledge became our servant, not our master.

We cannot say whether it worked. We knew that students enjoyed the whole experience and thought it worthwhile. On average, by the end of two terms, students had read twenty-seven books each, twenty-one of them 'properly'. Everyone had been intensively involved in some form of creative engagement with literature, often precisely directed. Might it not be possible that an approach such as this would lay a better foundation for both serious reading in life and academic literary study than any number of set books?

A Specimen Option List—Satire

ARDEN, John. *Serjeant Musgrave's dance.*
AUSTEN, Jane. *Northanger Abbey.*
BUTLER, Samuel. *The way of all flesh.*
BYRON, Lord George. *Don Juan* and *The vision of judgement.*
CHAUCER, Geoffrey. *The pardoner's tale.*

DICKENS, Charles. *Hard times.*
FIELDING, Henry. *Joseph Andrews.*
HARDY, Thomas. *Satires of circumstance.*
HELLER, Joseph. *Catch 22.*
HUXLEY, Aldous. *Brave new world.*
OPIE, Iona & Peter. *The lore and language of schoolchildren.*
ORWELL, George. *Animal Farm.*
PEACOCK, Thomas Love. *Nightmare Abbey.*
POPE, Alexander. *The rape of the lock.*
Private Eye magazine.
SHAW, George Bernard. *Major Barbara.*
SMITH, Edward Lucie (editor). *The Penguin book of satirical verse.*
STOPPARD, Tom. *The real inspector hound and After Magritte.*
SWIFT, Jonathan. *Gulliver's travels.*
THACKERAY, William Makepeace. *Vanity Fair.*
TROLLOPE, Anthony. *The way we live now.*
VOLTAIRE. *Candide* (Penguin translation).
WAUGH, Evelyn. *Decline and fall* and *The loved one.*

Plus any other appropriate material chosen by the students.

(Various forms of the course outlined here have been tried out in several different schools and colleges. The course as described here resulted from the intensive discussions of four tutors at what was then the City of Birmingham College of Education, now part of City of Birmingham Polytechnic. I am grateful to Miss V. Owen, Mrs J. Aldridge and Mr S. J. Burke (fellow tutors) and to many students for their contribution to these ideas. Also to Margaret Spencer for clarification of my contorted original version of this paper.)

Literature Teaching as an Educational Process

(a paper presented at the Naples Conference on the Teaching of Literature, December 1983. Though substantially rewritten, it incorporates material from the introduction to *Literature and Language Teaching*, Brumfit and Carter (eds.), Oxford University Press, forthcoming, 1985. It owes much to Roy Boardman's comments.)

The experience on which I base my observations in this paper includes teaching literature at primary, secondary and tertiary levels, to native and non-native speakers of English, and running training courses in a large number of countries. This experience has convinced me that it is rare for literature teaching to be seriously discussed in an educational context. Frequently it is taught because it always has been taught, in the way in which it always has been taught, and frequently it is subtly turned into cultural studies, or linguistics, or advanced English proficiency work, or history. My purpose here is to establish a number of key issues—as it were hooks onto which subsequent discussion may be hung. These issues seem to me to be crucial if we are to think clearly about what we are doing as teachers of literature.

Let me start by introducing a simple specification of literariness.

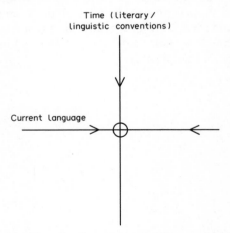

Any work of literature is a language act which exploits the resources of the time and place in which it is written. The horizontal axis reflects this characteristic. But unlike with other forms of writing, the vertical axis is equally important in literature. By the simple act of publishing a literary text, a writer cannot avoid being assessed as contributing to a class of texts which are already (for reasons it would be too complicated to explore here) accorded the status 'literature'. This class may be characterized by its fictionality, but it may also be characterized by a decontextualization which is implicit in fictionality but which can be found in any text which is read independently of its original transactional purposes. Thus

116

Gibbon's *Decline and Fall of the Roman Empire* is considered literature whether or not it is still historically sound, Keats's letters are read as literature and not solely as evidence for biographical study, and Orwell's essays are read independently of the arguments of their time to which they contributed. The literariness lies in the expectations of the reader, although, of course, fictional texts set up expectations of literariness more readily than do historical or political ones, for example.

Part of our developing the ability to read literature well must rely on increasing students' awareness of the context of any particular text on both these axes.

If we interpret literariness in any way similar to this we shall be able to specify more precisely what we are demanding of students—whether native or non-native speakers—who wish to become more proficient readers of literature. There seem to be four major factors to take into account.

1. *A language minimum.* While this is easy to refer to, it is hard to specify precisely, but it may be said in general that a non-native speaker who cannot read a text with at least the proficiency of a non-literary, uneducated but literate native-speaker (a fairly low level of reading ability, in fact) is probably not ready to respond to a text as literature. (I shall mention an exception to this claim later.)

2. *Cultural reference.* It is much easier to move from Italian to French or Spanish culture than to Chinese, or even Arab culture. Shared history, religion or literary tradition clearly contribute to the ease with which the function of cultural symbols operate across linguistic boundaries. Columbus is a symbolic figure for much of Europe: his cultural value is greater than simply a description of his acts. Similarly, a date like 1066 has greater resonance in Britain than in Italy.

3. *Literary convention.* There are similarities here with cultural reference. Clearly a convention like the sonnet form is cross-linguistic in Europe, but one which is modified by its various practitioners so that a good reader will benefit from having read other sonnets. The same principle applies to more abstract expectations, such as the conventions of courtly love, or the degree of moralization expected in traditions of Islamic poetry.

4. *Intellectual demands.* Within any educational system we have to recognize that works of literature may make intellectual demands as well as the others we have mentioned. To read Saul Bellow, for instance, requires a greater intellectual effort than to read Hemingway (to name two novelists of equal stature).

All these factors should be taken into account in considering what books are appropriate to what audiences of students. And in addition a further, purely pedagogic factor should be mentioned—length. Students with appropriate degrees of competence and understanding in all the four areas mentioned above may still benefit from working with a shorter rather than longer text of the right kind. Fatigue is a factor in misunderstanding.

Recognition of the role of factors such as these leads us to the consideration of issues of syllabus organization, the ordering of texts, and teaching methods. The rest of this paper will be concerned with these questions.

Is literature 'caught' or 'taught'?

If we see the teaching *of* literature as more than simply the use of literary texts in the classroom, we shall have to confront directly the implications of the notion of 'literary competence'. If, in practice, reading a literary text involves some sort of engagement by the reader beyond simply being able to understand the meanings of the utterances in the text, then we need to ask how this engagement is acquired. Traditional practice has normally been to include discussion and analysis of literary texts in class, and to assume that learners will in some way 'catch' the ability to read appropriately from the process of discussion and analysis in a fairly random way. Some thought may go in to the selection of texts, but the rest of the activity is frequently unplanned and random. And in many schools and colleges even the selection of texts is determined more by tradition or the interests of the teachers than by deliberate choice of those which are most suitable for the needs of the learners.

Now we need to recognize that random exposure is not necessarily a bad thing. Literary texts are complex objects and we can readily accept that their most important characteristics may be distorted or destroyed if a schematic and insensitive organization is imposed on a rich and subtle work of art. Good teachers have for many years selected works that they thought were accessible to their students and explored the implications of each work without trying to impose a rigid syllabus on the activity. And few people would expect us to be able to 'teach' someone to like a particular book.

But we can help students to avoid disliking a book simply because they misunderstand the conventions being used, or because the language is too difficult, or because the cultural references are inaccessible. Even if we assume that the development of sensitive and committed appreciation of literature is not going to be explicitly taught, we can still be as systematic as possible about the principles with which we operate. Only if we are can we expect new, inexperienced or overworked teachers to teach as effectively as their circumstances allow, for they will rely heavily on whatever publicly available help can be provided. Any successful teacher, therefore, has a responsibility to be as clear as possible about the principles—insofar as they can be publicly stated—on which that success has been based. At the same time, the process of making the bases of what we do as clear as possible will also help the private development and improvement of an individual teacher, for the clearer problems and difficulties are stated the more likely they are to be resolved.

In fact, the argument about what is caught and what is taught rests on a misunderstanding of the nature of teaching any complex subject. None of us teach anything worthwhile directly to students: we simply create the conditions for successful learning. Only in a trivial sense will we be able to train specific responses by direct intervention as with item-by-item question and answer. But we shall be able to demonstrate over a long period the process of responding to a varied range of works of literature and some of the infinite number of possible appropriate responses. In this sense, the teacher must provide the model towards which the students work—but only in general terms: we are not expecting students to replicate our responses in detail, only to develop their own, to move towards the kinds of responses we would expect of any sympathetic and reasonably knowledgeable adult reader. This is a model of behaviour which can only be caught; it certainly cannot be commanded or instructed.

The process of reading is a process of meaning-creation by integrating one's own needs, understanding and expectations with a written text. Each student will have different needs, understanding and expectations, so each student will derive slightly different messages from reading a particular book or poem. But the text itself will be constructed on the basis of conventions which may or may not be directly accessible to the student, and some of these conventions will, if misinterpreted, so distort the meaning that the text will be perceived as incomprehensible, or irrelevant. There is no point in leaving learners to grope their way towards understanding without direct intervention to clarify what might otherwise remain inaccessible for so long that they will give up literature in frustration if they are not helped. Nor, conversely, is there any point in insisting on detailed examination of points which, while obscure, do not impede initial response. There is no need to demand from non-native speakers of English a closer understanding of Dickens than we would expect of native-speakers, at least at the early stages of learning.

In other words, we should think in terms of suiting the literary demands that are made of students to their stage of development. We should have some notion of grading our activities. In practice, of course, all experienced teachers do this. But, unlike language teaching, for example, literature teaching does not seem to have had much serious discussion of the need to grade or the nature of appropriate grading. Consequently, many literature teachers resent the idea that the subtlety of their work should be crudely schematized by some sort of rigid grading system.

Yet this is not what is being asked for. All that is expected is that some principles should be established for sorting out priorities in teaching, to enable teachers and learners to work together more effectively. This will involve the teacher working with a whole range of different procedures, with the overall aim of allowing students to catch the ability to respond enthusiastically and appropriately to works of literature, but with subsidiary aims which will help students to learn specific points which will assist the larger aim.

The nature of literature syllabuses

If we are to talk at all clearly about literary syllabuses, we need to distinguish between a number of different reasons for using literary works in the classroom. In second and foreign language teaching there are at least three distinguishable major aims.

Many teachers use literature to assist the development of competence in the language. Although the texts being used are literary, and some of the responses of readers will be discussed in literary terms, the prime intention is to teach language, not literature, and the texts may be used as contexts for exemplification and discussion of linguistic items which have no bearing on the value of the work as literature. Sometimes there may be a major conflict in language pedagogy caused by the desire to use literary texts, and usually literary texts carry potential danger if the reasons for their use are not clearly thought through. Good literary texts are not thereby 'good style' for non-literary purposes, and they may indeed be misleading as linguistic material for learners with non-literary learning intentions.

A second reason for including literary texts is in order to teach 'culture'. It is claimed that studying literature enables us to benefit from the added interest of literary texts. But we cannot justify such material on the grounds that literature offers pictures of foreign life or samples of typical excellent language. Both of these claims are based on false theoretical positions.

A good language syllabus, then, may include literary texts, but will not necessarily do so. A syllabus intended to provide valuable cultural information will probably include literary texts, but should include a great deal of other information and sources of stimulus, including historical and journalistic material, samples of other art forms, and accounts of scientific and technical and sociological factors.

But of course literature is one major aspect of culture, and many people wish to study it in its own right. Furthermore it is more cheaply and easily accessible than many other cultural phenomena, and—because it is often responsive to international movements—it may be easier to comprehend than other more locally-based art forms. It is this kind of argument which, for many people, justifies the inclusion of literary courses in education. I would not wish in any way to oppose those who argue in this way. My only desire is to clarify the justifications for particular educational practices and traditions, so that inappropriate arguments are not advanced to defend and define particular practices.

The pure literature syllabus can be justified in its own right, educationally, but it should not be confused with syllabuses for the teaching of language or of culture. The criteria for the selection of texts to be used and the ordering most appropriate to the needs of students will vary depending on which type of syllabus is being adopted.

Some literary syllabuses, usually at advanced levels, may be primarily informative in intention, and may legitimately be concerned with the history of English literature, or of part of it. Others may be concerned with relating aspects of the English language literary tradition to particular local interests. There have, for example, been very interesting courses relating the American and Russian realist novel traditions. However, I would wish to argue that this kind of sophisticated language/literary discussion is best preceded by two independent stages of educational work. The first necessary preliminary is linguistic. There is a level of linguistic and cultural competence below which it is pointless trying to respond to works of literature.

Let me first of all modify this statement to the extent that I would accept that (for example) a German scholar, fully conversant with German, and perhaps some other literatures of the Romantic Period, might start studying English literature of the same period with scarcely any knowledge of English, and be able to go straight to Wordsworth, Keats or Byron with the aid of a bilingual dictionary. Such a person would be able to profit directly from a clear understanding of many shared frames of reference, and there are many examples of language learners who have operated successfully in this way. But they are not, of course, typical, and we are concerned with the role of literary studies in conventional education. So let us ignore those with initially high motivation or aptitude and concentrate on those whose motivation and aptitude can be developed through the educational experience.

For the typical secondary school learner a literary response cannot be given by a teacher; it can only arise out of the reading of a text. The problem, for both native and non-native speaking readers, is that a literary response only really starts when fluent reading has already been established. (It will of course develop out of other aesthetic experiences such as music, dance, listening to stories, and so on—but the adult response is in the last resort dependent on isolated reading for which certain preliminary abilities must have been developed.)

The first stage, then, is a minimum language competence. In the mother tongue, where there is a thriving literary tradition, this language competence will often develop side by side with story-telling, nursery rhymes, word games and personal narrative so that the switch to written mode will not entail a switch to a completely different set of premises, for literary structures influence speech as well as the other way round. In many parts of the world, where the mother tongue may be that of a primarily oral culture, the switch to written communication, that comes with schooling, may involve a much greater rhetorical shift. This is an aspect of literature teaching which has been little commented on, but it badly needs further study. We thus have three possible situations in school:

1. Students working in their mother tongue on literature, with a great deal of aesthetically structured speech and children's writing behind them.
2. Students working through a foreign or second language coming from a culture with a well-developed literary tradition, with which they are already slightly familiar (these will probably be a little older than those in 1 above).
3. Students working through a second language whose experience of artistically organized language is primarily oral, and whose culture may indeed have very different assumptions from those of western Europe about aesthetics and language.

I should perhaps emphasize that major writers and critics within the Western European tradition have originated from all three of these groups, though of course each bringing different perspectives to bear.

These three positions are all relative to each other, and few classes in schools will represent these in absolutely pure forms, but the distinctions clearly have some validity, and each type will require a slightly different syllabus. However, I would argue that there are fewer differences between them than might appear at first sight.

Even in the case of mother tongue students, few will come from homes where reading (in the sense that we are concerned with) is customary or necessary—and this will apply as much to 'middle class' or professional homes as to any others. Wide reading and appreciation of literature is thinly spread in all groups of the population. So we can assume that, in principle, we are developing a capacity which nearly all students need help with. Where there will be differences between the three groups is in the nature of their previous linguistic experience. Those in the first group will be developing greater linguistic and cultural (and cognitive) sophistication at the same time as they are being exposed to literature as a teaching subject. Those in the second will probably (and perhaps ideally should) meet the foreign literature when they have some understanding of literature as a phenomenon in their own culture, but with inevitably limited language, originally learnt with a more instrumental intention—usually—before they turned to literary texts. Those in the third group will have certainly learnt the language for educational and instrumental purposes before they have looked at sophisticated works of literature, but they will differ from the second group in their previous background in literature or any kind.

For all of these, though, we must conceive of the reading of works of literature as primarily an *experience*. And this experience presupposes the ability to gain access to it, at least in some crude sense. A person who has not the reading or comprehension fluency to make sense in general of the words on the page is not in a position to respond to the literariness of a text, and—in my view—the response (however limited or unrefined it may be) must precede the analysis or description of that response.

In crude terms, then, a literary syllabus can only start with a certain level of language or reading competence presupposed. That syllabus may take up from 'literary' elements in earlier reading or language work, but it can only start when considerations of literary significance are directly apprehendable by the learner. The literary syllabus itself (concerned primarily with enabling learners to respond to writing as literary rather than instrumental, pragmatically useful discourse) should have two broad stages, with the second one an option for those who wish to go on to become self-conscious about the process.

The first stage will be concerned with enabling students to 'experience' literature; the second will enable them to describe, explain, or otherwise 'account for' the experience. But, in my view, the error of much literature teaching is that, in practice, it reverses this process.

I shall not attempt at this stage to 'justify' the teaching of literature. Suffice it to say that for me, as for many teachers, the personal experience of reading major literature is sufficiently important for me to wish to communicate this need to my students and to help them develop the capacity to read for themselves in this way. Ultimately, perhaps, this is the only honest justification for any kind of teaching. Starting from this position, we can ask ourselves what particular groups of students must need if are to become committed readers of serious literature. We are avowedly socializing students into a community of serious readers—not with any necessary assumptions about what texts must be read, but with an assumption that the best reading matter will be approached through a tradition, in the sense of the accumulated experience of thousands of readers in the past and present who have been committed to reading, thinking about and discussing imaginative literature for the light it sheds on themselves and their position as human beings.

We do not start, then, with a programme of 'knowledge about' any particular literature, for we are not primarily concerned with external information. If students are to develop at some later date an understanding of particular historical traditions, they will only be able to do that reliably if they have already had some experience of genuine reading. We want to develop committed readers, who may read—say—Voltaire or Brecht or Solzhenitsyn or Greene or Achebe or Bellow. But we do not want to say to readers of novels that there are some of these writers that they should prefer. At a later stage there may be a place for arguments about which writers have most value in relation to particular philosophies or ideologies, but that argument should emerge from wide and varied reading. If our ambition is to produce as many students as possible who will read all these writers, and any others who could be included, we do not want to start with a course which relies on unnecessary limitation.

Consequently, the key criterion for a literature course is the accessibility for serious discussion and personal experience of the books being read to a particular group of students. Nor do we wish students to be taken through the books. Discussion is not a way of learning to read a book; it is something which analyses an experience already achieved, at least in part. So we need to select texts which students can have an initial reaction to unmediated by the teacher. Only then can we guide students' response rather than impose it from the outside.

Issues of grading are important and deserve further discussion but, for the moment it is enough to note that we need to be conscious of the intellectual level, the social and political expectations, the cultural presuppositions and the previous literary/ aesthetic experience, as well as the linguistic level of each class of students, as outlined at the beginning of this paper. In practice, such matters are often intuitively raised by teachers' discussions of which books have been successful in the past, but it is possible to be clear about the implications of such discussion only if we have a fairly clear idea of where we are going in a literature course and of what qualities students will normally bring to the course at the beginning.

If we are to teach literature effectively, then, we need to have some specification of the characteristics of typical learners when they start our course, and of what we want them to be like when they finish. Particularly, we need to recognize that we cannot claim to be teaching specific books; rather we are teaching attitudes and abilities which will be relevant to the reading of any major works of literature. To do this we should in addition have some view of what being a good reader entails, and of how the various kinds of classroom activity available to us will promote effective response. Although various people, including myself, have begun to discuss such questions, the discussion can only be preliminary, for the traditional high status of literature has—paradoxically—prevented the degree of analysis of aims, methods and objectives found in the discussion of other, less-favoured subjects.

'High' literature, literature, and reading

I have already suggested that the reading of literature is predicated upon a basic competence in general reading. In fact, many people, perhaps most even, in highly literate cultures, do a certain amount of reading as part of their daily life, but do not read any kind of imaginative literature at all. Many others do read, but would never think of reading any of the writers who have so far been referred to in this discussion. One of the advantages of a concern with literature as an attitude to texts rather than as a body of texts is that it is unnecessary to become involved with a discussion of 'highbrow' writers versus others. The capacity to read so that one is 'inside' the story is as necessary for Fielding or Dostoyevsky as it is for Arthur Haley, Barbara Cartland or Agatha Christie. The commitment for the literature teacher is to texts which can be discussed in such a way that the events, or characters, or anything else in the fictive world of the book are closely related to the personal needs of readers and learners as they attempt to define themselves and understand the human situation. The choice of books made by teachers, therefore, will reflect on profound and serious issues, and will draw upon the widely recognized tradition of 'serious' literature. But the methodology should encourage students to introduce into the discussion any books they read themselves which they themselves perceive to be relevant. Teachers of literature should not be concerned with the tradition because it is a tradition, but rather with books (which may or may not be part of the high tradition) that are directly needed by students at that stage of their literary development. These may be books which challenge assumptions, and should not normally be ones which merely reinforce local prejudices. But the issue of grading forces us to consider the relationship between colonial literatures to post-independence literature in third world countries, or literatures of marginal groups to mainstream literature in most countries. Ultimately the aim must be that readers should be willing and able to read the literature of many traditions, for only thus will it be an educational and value-challenging activity. But there is a great deal of sense in moving outwards from what is fairly fully understood, because it is based on local cultural assumptions, to literature of another class, region or period.

At the same time, it is dangerous to be too simplistic about what is accessible to whom. Shakespeare has been far more successful in Africa, where there is a strong tradition of oral rhetoric still alive, than in many urban centres in Britain, and students may find nineteenth-century literature closer to their own experience of how they live their lives than much contemporary work. The key question is how to provide students with a reading experience which enriches their perception of what it is to be human to a greater degree than other available experiences. It will be a long time before a more versatile piece of educational technology than the paperback book is invented, and there is no more easily available source for personal growth than serious literature. The tragedy is that, whether in mother tongue or foreign languages, literature remains inaccessible to so many people.

This argument suggests that we should think of literature syllabuses as incorporating three main phases, as in 2 above. Without minimum access in terms of linguistic, cultural and other expectations, it will not be possible to approach texts at all. From such minimum access the possibility of developing a literary experience will emerge. That is to say that students will read, enjoy and be willing to perceive a literary text as important in relation to their own understanding of themselves and the world. Without this response, in my own view, the third stage, explaining the

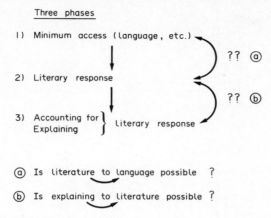

Three phases

1) Minimum access (language, etc.)

2) Literary response

3) Accounting for Explaining } Literary response

?? ⓐ

?? ⓑ

ⓐ Is literature to language possible ?

ⓑ Is explaining to literature possible ?

literary experience, will be impossible. Only when we have responded to literature should we be asked to understand literary theory, whether structuralist, deconstructionist or traditional. However, many scholars implicitly reject this view, and key questions for us to decide on are the extent to which literary response can move back into language development or explanation of literary response back into literary response itself. Those who use literature as a means of teaching language seem to suggest that we can move to 1 from 2. Those who use literary theory as a means of teaching literature seem to suggest we can move from 3 to 2. People committed to stylistics as a major device in literature teaching may be using it for either of these transitions. Whether or not they are justified will only be revealed by experience and further discussion.

Section Five:

TOWARDS A METHODOLOGY FOR TEACHER TRAINING

The final four papers are all concerned with making sense of teacher training for language teachers. The first paper contains a practical exemplification of an integrated scheme for teaching methods in EFL. In this scheme, practical experience, basic theoretical concepts and student activities are combined as fully as possible so that learning becomes inductive rather than deductive, particularly in the early stages. This scheme was in fact developed in a workshop in Mexico City, but it seems sensible to give a specific illustration of the principles, even if that means having items that are local in time or place. In fact, this scheme has been used as a basis for development and modification in other parts of the world. I am most grateful for the contribution of the teachers at the Escuela Normal Superior in Mexico City for their ideas and effort.

The second paper tries to identify the general principles underlying our work in initial teacher training at the University of London Institute of Education—and, I would claim, in all my work in teacher education. The third paper also derives from the London Institute, but essentially (though this is not how I formulated it at the time) involves applying the concept of fluency, as in the second paper of this book, to microteaching. The paper gives a detailed discussion of an intensive micro-teaching programme which breaks with the assumptions of the original, classic microteaching model. Finally, in a paper written with a friend, ex-student and colleague, Richard Rossner, we examine the context of teacher education in terms of the organization of the profession. Such a collaboration (in which the first idea came from my co-author, but which takes up some of the themes in the last paper of my previous collection of papers for Pergamon) seems a fitting way to end this collection.

Integrating Theory and Practice

(from 'Teacher Training', ed. S. Holden, *Modern English Publications*, 1979)

Despairing teacher trainers frequently remark that teaching is both an art and a science. Usually, resort to this cliché comes when students are pressing for explicit answers to questions which cannot be answered explicitly. Teaching is a science in that it is possible to make explicit and systematic generalizations about it, and to submit these generalizations to some sort of empirical test. It is an art in that no objective statement of procedures, no algorithm however precise, will enable good teaching to occur with any teacher and any class. One of the biggest difficulties in the initial training of teachers is to persuade students that there are no easy answers, that some vitally important questions cannot be given objective answers, and—in EFL particularly—that specific teaching techniques are inseparably bound up with issues of educational principle. Language, in short, is too complex an activity to be trained simply, and social pressures to produce 'scientific' solutions must be resisted: the main value of scientific procedures in language teaching is metaphorical.

This appears to be a strong statement, and it will indeed be modified later in this article, but it is worth putting it in a strong form at the outset, for all of us, teachers and teacher trainers alike, are professionally committed to the process of useful simplification. The danger is that we shall end up by being not simple but simplistic.

I hope to argue here that the problem of integrating theory and practice centres on the need to recognize what questions can and can not be answered objectively. I also want to make a claim for teacher training courses not trying to do some of the things which have been seen as central to their activities: particularly, they should not claim that we know how learners learn or how good teachers teach. The reason for insisting on this limitation is that we do, in fact, know too little to be able to generalize efficiently. Of course we should offer what we do know, but we should avoid making claims, for the sake of simplicity, which are not justified by our current state of understanding.

What is practice?

If we are talking about riding a bicycle, we are unlikely to refer to anything less than getting on the bicycle and attempting to go as practical learning. Teaching, however, is a much more complicated combination of activities than riding a bicycle and the analogy soon breaks down when we apply it to education. The nearest practice in normal teacher training courses to bicycle riding is the extended period of more or less full-time teaching in a school found in conventional initial training courses. All other types of practical activity are, to some degree, unreal exercises. Such exercises include teaching one day a week, or single classes, in schools (unreal because the teaching is fragmented so that the student may be teaching individual lessons in isolation, or as a visitor rather than a member of the school), microteaching with real students (unreal both because the teaching is limited in

129

scale and because the students are not there to learn anything as part of a genuine course), peer teaching (unreal *because* it is peer), and casual simulations on an ad hoc basis during methods classes. All of these have their value, and they represent various stages in the process of grading contact between trainee student and the full situation. The difficulty is that the false elements in each of these situations are often perceived by students to be enormously important. They frequently find it difficult to work from the pseudo-situation to the real one, and the more the tutor tries to explain, the greater the risk of explanations becoming a substitute for any direct experience at all.

There are, of course, many other forms of practical activity which relate—directly or indirectly—to teaching. These vary from work of direct classroom applicability, like preparation of lesson plans or teaching materials, to practical work based on theoretical discussion which has bearing on language teaching problems, like making phonemic transcriptions of the speech of typical learners or analysing videotaped lessons. However, the purpose of all of these is to enable the students to understand principles of some kind which will then need to be tested against his own classroom experience. It is this testing against classroom experience which will be promoted by the good training course.

What is theory?

Because language use is such a complex activity, and because it involves the personality and social expectations of the user so intimately, the language teacher must be adaptable. In the last resort it is the individual learner who learns, not some generalized principle of learning theory. Yet language teachers have to be adaptable in some way which enables them to be most efficient. They must operate according to principles, and these should be sufficiently clearly stated for discussion to be possible, whether that involves empirical verification of statements of fact, logical procedures to examine arguments, or merely identification of which principles are assertions which cannot be tested because they are being advanced as axiomatic. No practical problems are ever solved without recourse to principles of some kind. If they are unstated, the risk is that they will be unexamined. In the end, teacher training must be about the principles for teaching rather than what to do in particular circumstances, for no two sets of circumstances are the same and there are few rules for all occasions, and those that there are vacuous (e.g. 'Don't stand in front of the blackboard when you have written on it'.) This suggests that the best teacher training course must therefore be based on principles rather than practice. And immediately it is possible to imagine cries of horror in response to such a statement. However, the principles do not exist as abstract generalizations; they only have value insofar as they are seen to be based on successful practice and insofar as they produce successful practice.

Design of a satisfactory teacher training course, then, will be crucially dependent on the way in which principles are related to realized classroom activity. Establishing a satisfactory relationship then becomes a methodological problem, one of organization rather than content.

Possible ways of organizing a course

In an ideal world, there would be many ideal teachers. Students could then be allocated to teachers who were performing more or less full duties in schools, could work alongside them over a long period, and would see principles being exemplified in practice systematically in a real situation. Unfortunately there are more students than there are ideal teachers, and there are strong administrative difficulties to prevent widespread apprenticeship—though the possibilities have been explored far less than they should have been by educational authorities. Nonetheless, the tutor on a training course has to fulfil some of the role of the ideal teacher, and should be able to provide a living exemplification of the integration of theory and practice. The tutor will have another role to play, however, and this is the main feature which distinguishes a good teacher from a good teacher trainer. The tutor must be able not merely to illustrate, but also to *discuss*, good teaching principles. There are many good teachers who are apparently incapable of being self-conscious about their procedures. But without the ability to discuss, communication between tutor and student must proceed entirely intuitively. And, while intuitive communication is both inevitable and necessary, it cannot be sufficient, because—by definition—it cannot be discussed or analysed, and will therefore never be assessed objectively. A long-term apprenticeship may lead to understanding by osmosis, but courses of less than several years must rely largely on more overt procedures; furthermore (and more importantly) we have no way of telling whether the seeds being implanted through intuitive learning are good or bad ones until it is too late. Thus, while recognizing the value of close and indefinable contacts between tutors and students, we must concentrate most strongly on the aspects of teaching which can be objectively discussed.

This line of argument suggests that the role of the tutor will be crucial. Tutors will be most honest when they present themselves as examples of people attempting to integrate theory and practice, and when they show as objectively as possible what the difficulties are in doing this. If they imply that they know how other people, such as their students, should teach in specific situations, they will be demonstrating either arrogance or (more likely) insufficient appreciation of the intimate relationship between teaching and individual personality. A tutor can be a good example, but not a model.

The best course will provide many opportunities for the tutors to illustrate the process of simultaneously being principled and practical, many opportunities for the discussion and objective assessment of this process, and many opportunities for students to work in this way themselves. What sort of organization will best provide such opportunities?

First, since a training course is not aiming to produce either linguists or educational theorists, it will be an *integrated* course. The use of theory will be explictly related to the need to solve practical problems. Second, whether or not all theory leads direct to school experience, it should lead direct to *practical activities* (i.e. activities performed by the students). Third, students should be free to remain themselves within the course structure; the course is about *being themselves*, not about becoming somebody else. This final point is important, for 'brilliant' teacher trainers probably do more harm than good, and brilliant demonstration lessons put off many students who see them as setting an unattainable standard. Anyway, teacher training is not about brilliance—the talented need it least—it is about helping the initially less talented to become as effective as possible.

To deal with the last two points first. The kinds of activity which most enable students both to be practical and themselves include the school practice period and certain sorts of simulated classroom situation. What has been called 'exploratory' microteaching (Carver and Wallace, 1977) in which the tutor concentrates the discussion on any major teaching ideas or strategies which emerge from the lesson (which may be as long as twenty minutes or more) gives an excellent opportunity to ask questions like, 'At that point in the lesson, what particular options were available?' 'Which one was chosen?' 'What else could have been done.' 'What effect would that have had?' and so on. Similarly, seminars held close to the school teaching situation will enable students to reteach to their peers lessons which they have just taught in school, and these can be interrupted, analysed and alternative possibilities explored most fruitfully. With both of these, the teaching is an example to be used as a base for discussion, not a lesson to be evaluated and 'corrected' in any way. But through these two procedures a more or less active teaching experience can be subjected to intensive and practical discussion. Alternative approaches all have some disadvantages. Using videotaped lessons, for example, does not provide the chance to discuss something with the teacher, nor to look at something which has been experienced rather than observed. Observing real lessons is valuable, but only a few people can be present without disrupting the class, and discussion often has to be long after the event.

At the same time, more structured work also has a value, both formal microteaching, and use of VTR lessons for the purpose of analysis and comment, as well as other kinds of activity which have been referred to above. Nor will the tutor's role be merely that of refusing to make value judgements; clearly the tutor's experience should have led to *some* views about preferred approaches. But the major value of the tutor will lie in students having someone available who is simultaneously well read, experienced in a variety of situations, and aware of the limitations of discussion. Training can help prepare a teacher, but it cannot make one, and no-one should expect a student to be a competent teacher immediately on leaving a training course. Students who are must be either very talented or already experienced. What training can try to do is to create an attitude of being organized, of always probing and trying to improve, of refusing to follow fashions without good reason—in short, of informed, optimistic scepticism. The course will thus be providing the *basis* for the development of skills, but these skills can only be developed by teachers while they are actually teaching. It will also be attempting to promote attitudes to students, colleagues and the process of thinking about teaching which will enable continuous professional development to take place. It is this which is the justification of the course, and the technical matters are simply the means to this end.

As an illustration of the possible shape of an integrated scheme, an outline is given below of an integrated syllabus for basic teacher training. This was originally prepared in 1976 by teachers at the Escuela Normal Superior in Mexico City, during a workshop which I ran for the British Council. It does illustrate one possible design for a syllabus which, in combination with the procedures outlined in the article, could be an effective basis for training EFL teachers. There are four phases. In the first, the emphasis is on practical skills, but these are integrated with specific basic theoretical concepts which will be systematically introduced into the discussion. The second phase concentrates on organization for specific teaching levels, with emphasis again on practical work with basic theoretical cross referencing. Phase three for the first time looks at theoretical principles, but by now there is a great deal of practical work to refer back to, and phase four adds basic information which should be provided for teachers as they embark on their professional careers.

BASIC SCHEME FOR METHODS COURSE
N.B. *These stages show an order but they are not time units.*

Phase 1
PRACTICAL TECHNIQUES
A. Listening & Speaking; B. Reading; C. Writing

Stage	Practical Experience	Basic Theoretical Concepts	Student Activity
	A.—LISTENING & SPEAKING		
1	'Lesson' in a foreign language with presentation, choral, individual and pairs practice shown	Three levels of language: sound grammar meaning	They are 'taught' the lesson and will *discuss* it in groups, guided by controlled questions.
2	Organizing choral and individual class practice	L_1 & L_2 differences	a *Practise* using choral and individual techniques. b *Discuss* learning method.
3	Pairs activity: a) separate pairs b) simultaneous pairs	'Communicative' teaching	a *Practise* techniques, and b *Discuss* rationale for the procedure.
4	Presentation skills	The teachers' use of the classroom and available resources (media)	a *Prepare* presentations in group. b *Practise* on peers or on a real class.
5	Contextualizing meaning, including introducing dialogues	The nature of a context	*Practise* introduction of appropriate language sequences.
6	Remedial techniques: pronunciation a) recognition	Phonological problems	*Practise* techniques.
7	Remedial techniques: pronunciation b) production	Phonological problems (continued)	*Practise* techniques.
8	Remedial techniques: oral structure	Audio-lingual learning principles	*Practise* drilling techniques.
9	Communication: Aural comprehension	Varieties of language: accent/dialect	*Practise* reading and writing questions for oral passages.
10	Communication: games	Motivation in the language class	*Play* games.
11	Communication: discussion/conversation	Fluency vs. accuracy. Aims of oral work	*Devise* and *practise* techniques.

B. READING

12	Applying oral techniques to reading stimuli	Correspondence of English sound and writing systems contrasted with Spanish	Student practice.
13	Remedial techniques for reading aloud	Correspondence of English sound and writing systems contrasted with Spanish	Student practice.
14	Basic reading procedures. Sentences and longer sequences	Skills or lack of skills. Transfer to English	*Practise* effective reading aloud of longer passages; voice projection.
15	Using oral questions on reading texts	Nature of comprehension	*Draft* part of lesson plan with questions on a given text.
16	Using written questions on reading texts	Possible causes for comprehension errors	*Prepare* and *test* and *revise* questions on a given text.

C. WRITING

17	Techniques for introducing writing at sentence level	Writing as a learning device	*Play* memorization games with and without help by being allowed to write.
18	Techniques based on textbook materials	The role of the textbook in class activity	*Teach* mini-lessons in small groups with textbook.
19	Oral preparation techniques (for writing)	Integration of skills	*Plan* preparation in groups. Some to *demonstrate* to whole class.
20	Controlling techniques	Justification for controlled work	*Write* several types of controlled writing exercises.
21	Guiding techniques (planning for class)	Methodological sequencing	*Draft* complete lesson plan for guided composition lesson.
22	Techniques for pupils' correction	Cognitive versus behaviourist language learning theories	*Answer* one writing exercise (Stage 20), anticipating typical errors, and *propose* pupil-centred correction technique.
23	Remedial techniques for written errors	Error analysis	*Correct* and *classify* errors in a given passage. *Discuss* in groups.

Phase 2
APPROACHES BY TEACHING LEVEL

Stage	Practical Experience	Basic Concept	Student Activity
24	Presentation of lesson plan (Part A) Pre-class activities	Selections sequencing	*Discuss* and *prepare* Stage A of a lesson plan by group.
25	Presentation of lesson plan (Part B) In-class activities	Objectives	*Discuss* and *prepare* Stage B of a lesson plan.
26	Division of a lesson plan into class plans	Motivation through variety of activities	*Divide* lesson plans into class plans.
27	Application of practical techniques (Phase I) to first grade syllabus	The Role of a Syllabus	*Prepare* lesson plans for the structures in the first grade syllabus with reference to existing textbooks.
28	Application of practical techniques to second grade syllabus content. (Additional and more complex techniques: pupils prepare dialogues, dramatization of dialogues, communicative activities, picture-story composition.)	Objectives	*Prepare* lesson plans for the structures in the second grade syllabus with reference to existing textbooks.
29	Application of practical techniques to third grade syllabus content. (Additional, more complex communicative activities. Extensive reading, written composition; messages, letters, etc.)	Self-evaluation in relation to lesson planning	*Prepare* lesson plans for the structures in the third grade syllabus with reference to existing textbooks.
30	Teaching adults	Age factor	*Discuss* use of appropriate materials.
31	Advanced work: more complex techniques	E.S.P. and English for Vocational Purposes	*Discuss* appropriate materials.
32	Evaluation and testing pupils' performance	Purpose and function of evaluation	*Practise* evaluation techniques in relation to syllabus and available materials.

Phase 3
ANALYSIS OF METHODOLOGICAL PROCEDURES

Stage	Basic Theoretical Concepts	Reference to previous Practical Stages	Student Activity
33	Different Methods Eclectic Method	I-A-1	Assignment in reading on different methods. Group discussion of techniques pertaining to each method. Summary by teachers.
34	Aims and goals of Language. Reasons for teaching English related to aims and goals of language work	II-28, 31	Group discussion of Basic Concept. Summary by teacher. Reading assignment.
35	Problems of language teaching in Mexico. Mixed-ability groups	I-A-2, 4, 6, 7, 10 I-B-12, 13, 14, 15, 16 I-C-23 II-26, 30, 31	Reading assignment Group discussion and conclusions.
36	Pupil's characteristics (variables)	I-A-10 II-26, 30	Reading assignment. Group discussion and summary.
37	Differences in learning L_1 and L_2 (individual differences in learning)	I-A-2, 6, 7, 10 I-C-17, 21, 22 II-24, 25, 26, 28, 30	Reading assignment. Group discussion and summary.
38	Need for standard model	I-A-9, 11 II-24	Listening to different forms of standard English (native speakers). Group discussion and conclusions.
39	Differences between Surface and Deep Structure	I-A-3, 5 I-B-15, 16	Analysis of text and dialogues. Discussion on meaning.
40	Syntactic Analysis of L_2	I-A-1 I-B-16 I-C-23 II-24, 27	Analysis of basic structures and systems of language description.
41	Error Analysis of Syntax	I-A-1, 2 I-B-16 I-C-20, 23 II-24	Reading assignment. Error analysis of their own compositions and speech and that of pupils.
42	Error Analysis of phonological problems both of pupils and students	I-A-1, 2, 6, 11 I-B-12, 13 I-C-20 II-24	Reading assignment. Error analysis of their own speech and that of pupils.
43	Phonetics. Its use in the classroom	I-A-1, 2, 6, 7, 11	Discussion and conclusions.
44	Direct method. (Use of L_2 in the classroom)	I-A-3, 4, 5, 11 I-C-18, 21, 22 II-24, 25, 28	Reading assignment. Group discussion on the Direct Method and its contribution to foreign language learning.

45	Rationale for the use of Audio-lingual techniques	I-A-3, 4, 5, 8, 11 I-C-18, 21, 22 II-24, 25, 28	Reading assignment. Group discussion on the Audio-lingual Method and its contribution to foreign language learning.
46	Influence of teacher's personality and attitude. (Basic characteristics)	I-A-4, 10 II-26, 29	Group discussion and conclusions after observation of real classes.
47	Textbooks Analysis	I-A-3, 4, 5, 10 I-C-17, 18, 19, 21, 22 II-24, 26, 27, 31	Comparative analysis based on criteria of textbooks in use in secondary schools.
48	Language as Communication	I-A-1, 3, 5, 9, 11 I-B-15 I-C-19 II-25, 28, 31	Group discussion and conclusion.

Phase 4
ORGANIZATION AND BACKGROUND INFORMATION

49	The role of English and English teaching in Mexico.—Statistics.
50	International support of the Teaching of English as a Foreign Language. Organization of English Language Teaching information. Bibliography.

Creating Coherence in ELT Teacher Training

(from R. R. Jordan (ed.), *Case Studies in ELT*, Collins, 1983)

This article addresses itself to a problem which I have found both the most important and the most difficult in teacher training: preventing the course from being a mish-mash of odds and ends which are presented separately so that the responsibility for integration is entirely left with the inexperienced students. So many courses consist of bits of psychology, bits of linguistics, methodological tips and chunks of teaching practice, with the result that students rarely see for themselves the process of integration which by implication they themselves are supposed to exemplify. Yet it is possible for the attitude of the teaching staff, the administration and organization of the course, the choice of content, and the teaching procedures used to demonstrate and reflect the concerns that students are expected to be aware of in their own school or college teaching.

To achieve such a result, it is not enough simply to manufacture an attractive and apparently coherent package. Integration will ultimately reside in the behaviour of the trainee students, so whatever package is devised must be specifically adjustable to the very varied needs of particular types of student. The two problems of integration and adaptation to the different personalities of students are inseparable. Looking back on attempts to achieve satisfactory integration on a whole range of teacher training courses, from summer schools to B.Ed. duration, I can see a number of underlying principles that have emerged from our practice. It will probably be most helpful if these principles are discussed in themselves, so that readers can relate them to their own situations and needs, but I shall illustrate their practical implications with reference to the one-year Post-Graduate Certificate in Education in the ESOL Department of London University Institute of Education.

Principle I: Openness of procedure

We considered that in many important respects the teacher training process could be made an image of the language teaching process, so that all aspects of our activity in planning, teaching, evaluating and adapting the course were made as open as the university regulations allowed. As far as possible we justified the decisions we made to students with reference to our own discussions, pointing out the compromises that were necessary as a result of administrative and legal constraints, the needs of individual students and individual staff, financial limits and timetabling problems. As a result of this, we hoped, students would see from the start that teaching takes place in response to a range of often conflicting interests, and that they themselves were only one of the factors to be taken into account. We hoped also that, by making it clear that a course in ELT methodology taught by several tutors necessarily compromised the beliefs of each of the tutors, we would compel an immediate recognition of variety in approaches to language teaching. We wished to open up the inevitable problems of the relationship between principle and practice from the very beginning of the course, as well as reveal the mechanisms by which the course had been constructed and the processes of planning and teaching.

Openness of procedure was achieved partly by an agreement among tutors that we would encourage discussion of this kind, and initiate it wherever appropriate, partly by specific handouts explaining the basis for parts of the course, and partly by regular formal and informal opportunities for feedback and collaboration by students in the evaluation and planning of parts of the course.

But there were of course some limits to openness. Any group of three or four tutors varies in its competencies and interests. The personal assessments of individual strengths and weaknesses that contribute to serious planning cannot be spelt out in a completely open way without creating insecurity among both students and staff, and no single tutor could make an unbiased analysis, anyway. But there was no reason why students should not understand that variations in interests, or even motivations, by tutors had to be taken into account. The principle could be referred to without coyness, even if specific illustrations were avoided as being both tactless and inevitably biased and subjective. In as many ways as possible we were self-conscious about the course, in public, all the time.

Principle II: Integration of planning

The methodology course was taught by either three or four tutors, depending on the number of students we were allowed to take. It was taken as axiomatic that all of us should know everything that all the others did. In the first year of the redesigned course we all sat through everything, gruelling in time though that was. New tutors would do the same in their first year. Furthermore, all planning of everything was scrutinized by everyone, until it was clear that we had all defined our own places in relation to the contributions of everyone else. As a result of this, it was possible for all tutors to integrate different parts of the course on the basis of direct experience, and to present in their discussions with students more than a partial view of our activities. Furthermore this ensured that none of us was as ignorant of areas outside our specialities at the end as at the beginning. This was particularly important as our PGCE methodology course includes a substantial amount of basic linguistic and phonetic work which needed great care in integrating with the practical work. Even though we never achieved as close an integration as we hoped for, the effort of attempting to enabled us to clarify our perceptions of each other and thus to broaden our understanding of language teaching itself.

Integration could only be achieved by hard work, both in making time to specify syllabuses in advance, indicating inter-relationships, and discussing them together, and also in attending other people's sessions. This does seem to be one area in which flair may be valuable but sheer hard grind is unavoidable. Without such effort, however, we would have been unable ourselves to be seen to be integrating principle and practice, and we would inevitably have taught partly at cross-purposes to each other. Now, if we disagree, we are able to point out that we do so, with reasons, and thus present a coherent but not monolithic picture of the profession.

Principle III: Continuous feedback

During the period we are discussing, PGCE numbers varied between 45 and 60 students. Consequently informal feedback mechanisms were not enough. We did of course have frequent (at least twice weekly) meetings with tutors at which urgent matters would inevitably be raised within a group of not more than fifteen students. However, we also had termly sessions of a morning or afternoon which were officially designated 'feedback sessions' to which students were encouraged to bring preselected comments on the course in all its aspects. It was also staff policy to be as informally open as possible on all occasions, but teaching commitments on other courses and other responsibilities clearly limited the value and effectiveness of this policy without more overt attempts to get formal responses. Other mechanisms for feedback included a detailed questionnaire at the end of the year, in which questions were asked specifically on all separate aspects of the course, as well as broader issues, and the general departmental staff–student meetings held once a term which enabled representatives from each course to meet each other.

Such mechanisms as these are widespread. But they deserve some comment, for they do raise problems. In some ways they provided us with very useful suggestions and support. We were able, for example, to obtain comments in advance on modifications to the course proposed for the following year, and in retrospect on modifications initiated at the request of students from the previous year. In this way the role of a syllabus, and of a tradition of particular teaching procedures, became clearer, for often students one year restored what had been abolished the previous year, or asked insistently for changes which we too would have liked to operate but which were too expensive or administratively too radical to be accepted by the university or government. On the other hand, we had serious problems in analysing the status of the criticisms we received. Were we creating a climate in which criticisms, however little felt, *had* to be produced because there was a timetable slot for them? It was not uncommon for students to semi-retract in private what they had said in public, or to dissociate themselves from what others had said, on the grounds that an official feedback session is asking for the time to be filled with demands for change, however slightly felt they are. Yet this does seem to be the lesser of the evils. Without official slots for comment, there remains a risk that genuine complaints may not be aired, and perhaps feedback must not merely occur, but must also be seen to occur.

At the same time, it is important to stress that we did genuinely act on suggestions and complaints wherever practicable. Yet this too has its dangers. People come on courses in order to receive education or training from people who appear to know what they are doing. We had to be careful not to imply that we were passively waiting to be told what students wanted. One part of our own expertise was that we probably, by training and experience, knew more of the options available than any one trainee teacher. Part of our role had to be extending their awareness of the questions to be asked, and to enable them to question some of their own answers to the questions they were already asking. Feedback is part of a process of consultation, but it could not become a substitute for planning. One of the most useful roles of formal feedback sessions was to reveal to students the wide variety of their own demands and needs, so that they became increasingly aware of the need for a general syllabus which could be individualized within boundaries imposed by finance and time.

Principle IV: Variety of teaching procedure

We have, through our feedback mechanisms, encountered students who insist on nothing but lectures, nothing but groupwork, nothing but individualized learning packs, and—in at least one case—nothing but daily individual tutorials! However, it is not simply to accommodate differing demands that we would consider variety of teaching procedure as a basic principle. People are varied and adaptable, and their needs vary from time to time and place to place. Often we do not ourselves know what we can do and what we can benefit from. Since teachers particularly need to recognize the enormous variety of learning strategies that language learners can employ successfully, they must both be aware of variety, and be willing to be self-conscious about the uses and abuses of the many possible modes of class organization. In spite of widespread doubts about the lecture mode, there are some educational virtues that are unique to that form. Only in a lecture can students be exposed to a demonstration of the process of argumentation, by one person, which can adjust itself to the needs and level of the audience according to its responsiveness. Much thinking has to be done on one's own, and good lectures can—in moderation—perform this, and other useful functions. So we build in some lectures, some workshops, some discussion groups, some individualized material, some library access work (visual and recorded), some peer-teaching and microteaching, and so on. It is true, of course, that not all the lectures or seminars are good—we cannot live up to our best intentions all the time; but without demonstrations of the strengths and weaknesses of a whole range of teaching procedures—coupled with the discussion of these—it is difficult to see how students can extend their experience of the educational possibilities available. A similar point may apply also to evaluation procedures, though this is less often in the control of tutors on a course. People are as good as their best performance, and not everyone performs well in interaction, or on projects, or without a strong and unreal incentive like a formal examination. It seems unfair to reward only one type of worker.

Principle V: Emphasis on what you do as a teacher

Teachers do many things other than teach, but the practical goal of training is to enable students to be good teachers. This requires a predominant emphasis on classroom performance—hence our eleven weeks or so of full-time teaching practice in schools in London and Madrid—but it also requires that students evaluate and adapt textbooks, plan lessons and schemes of work, watch each other teach and talk about what they have seen, make and mark tests, and so on. A great deal of the course must consist of doing these things, so our main mode of activity has been through workshops of various kinds. But of course many of these are not the real thing, and students are aware of this. Much of our work must necessarily be simulation: planning lessons for classes that will not actually be taught or teaching lessons to each other rather than to real students. What is crucial for integration is the feeling among students that the focus is right—on the practical activity rather than the under-pinning theory. I have discussed elsewhere (in this volume, and in Brumfit, 1980) the integration of theory with practice, but it is worth emphasizing the role of language study here, for this is an aspect of theory which is going to become more and more important. Few newcomers to the language teaching profession have had much formal study of language, and some terminology for the description of language learning processes and for the diagnosis of error and variation is necessary. We have tried a variety of ways of integrating this work with practical needs, but never to the complete satisfaction of our clientele. It does need to be emphasized to trainees that understanding the codes through which we communicate is an essential and practical activity of all efficient teachers, and that thinking about language on the basis of data provided for or by the classroom cannot be avoided.

Principle VI: Lack of rigidity

Nothing we have done has been applied wholesale. We have not tried to individualize by pigeon-holing students into a classification of 'types', because we do not believe that anyone is exclusively and consistently any one type. Rather we have attempted to ensure that everyone receives some experience of everything, without feeling forced to operate through one particular mode of learning or interaction pattern. There is quite a strong 'core' methodology course with a content which we claim all language teachers should cover if they are to be competent in their profession. But *how* an individual wishes to approach this content, and which parts of it are to be concentrated on—as well as which of a range of options are to be pursued beyond the core—is not dictated. Most particularly, I would want to argue that we have no rigidity in our interpretation of what is a good teaching style. Not only should a teaching style be determined partly by the traditions and needs of the learners, but also it should derive from the personality of the teacher. Everyone teaches in a different way because we teach as the people we are. On teaching practice, and in microteaching sessions, we have tried a variety of ways of introducing students to the options available in techniques, methods and materials. But the prime purpose of both these activities is to provide us as tutors with data to work on. I have sometimes said to students that I can describe many aspects of bad teaching, but I cannot describe good teaching: I simply know it when I see it. And I would certainly want to argue strongly that the tutor's job is to take the teaching that students do on teaching practice, and help them to do what they are setting out to do as well as possible, on their own terms, while at the same time helping them to evaluate the worth of the objectives they have felt able to choose. It is not the responsibility of the tutor, or of anyone else, to say 'Good teaching is like this', for it is infinitely varied. Furthermore, we need to show students how best to use the capacities they have, not to aspire to those which others have developed—at least at the beginning of their careers.

As a result of this, we may lose in charisma, for we are not apparently selling a marvellous new package, but we should gain in honesty.

Principle VII: Uncertainty

All the principles that have so far been outlined lead up to this one. The only thing I am prepared to say with certainty about language teaching is that there are no simple answers. All teachers, and especially those at the beginnings of their careers, need support and security. But they are much more likely to get this from an honest appraisal of the problems than from a pretence that simple panaceas exist. People learn languages successfully through rote learning, translation, reading, impromptu communication, carefully prepared recitation, creative writing, role-plays, physical activities or any combinations of these or other procedures. The public would like (wouldn't we all?) a method that 'taught' a language in a week's light effort, and there will always be temptations to market instant solutions. But for full language learning, in order to mix on easy terms with competent speakers of a foreign language, the path will be long, the effort considerable, and the means unpredictable. Teachers can help this process, but they cannot specify the process in detail in advance for each learner. Expertise consists of recognizing this, and then trying to be as principled as possible.

The organization and structure of the course relies on a belief that effective teaching, in the real world of institutions and politics, student demands and teachers' needs, will necessarily have to build piecemeal on the traditions, good and bad, of the past. To do this well demands that the past and present states of language teaching are examined, sympathetically but sceptically, in the light of the best available knowledge of the process of language learning and language use. The course does not therefore ignore theory, but it treats it as necessarily transitional. The world changes as people change. Our understanding changes and improves, but it will never be complete or final. We, and the teachers we train, have to operate with uncertainty, because that is the human condition, and it is no service to create security by means of fictions. But out of this sense of uncertainty can arise a confidence, if our procedures and example are co-operative, informed and as rigorous as possible, for we are training teachers to work well in a world which will necessarily change, without providing false hopes of success and without recommending a cynical, passive desire to merely survive.

*   *   *   *   *

All these basic principles, which have appeared after teaching and designing many courses, not as axioms before the process started, have one major objective: to provide a course which concentrates neither on theory nor practice, but on the relationship between them. A teacher who has a vast fund of techniques but who never thinks about the principles underlying them will not be able to create new ones nor adjust them to changing circumstances. And even more worrying is the teacher who has learnt about principles without ever having experienced their application in the classroom. What is more, it is perfectly possible for classroom practice to occur quite independent of application of theory. But a teacher who is constantly trying to improve will of necessity be looking for the basis for improvement, the underlying generalizations which derive from successful practice. Experience in training of the process of generalizing from experience in order to adapt and improve, together with experience of speculating on the basis of new ideas and applying those to the classroom provides a firm basis for professional education. To obtain this, though, time is necessary. Becoming a good teacher demands extensive development over a long period. Perhaps in an ideal world we might have two years of training in and out of college, combined with at least another year in the position of an apprentice. In the world as it is, we have to make do with much less, but the responsibility of teaching is too great to be left to the odd few weeks of training that are so often all that is available. The principles outlined here are worthwhile for short or long courses, initial training or in-service—with some minor modifications. But they are primarily useful because they force the process of teacher training to present a coherent model without presenting a dictatorial one.

A Seven-day Microteaching Programme for EFL Teachers

(from Cripwell and Geddes (eds.), *Microteaching and EFL Teacher Training*, EFL Department Working Papers 1, 1979, University of London Institute of Education)

In this short paper I want to describe the procedures which I have developed for microteaching with students on the Postgraduate Certificate in Education during a short, intensive period which is set aside for microteaching work. Tutors work in their own way with groups of about fifteen students, all of whom have at least two years' teaching experience before coming on the course.

Many over-strong claims have been made for the value of microteaching. I would like to make limited claims for it on the following bases:

(i) By peer teaching in a micro-situation we are able to isolate certain aspects of the teaching situation from the presence of genuine students; thus certain techniques and abilities can be concentrated on in a comparatively pure form.

(ii) We are provided with as live as possible a context for the discussion of teaching problems (real students would be unfair on the students, for they will always have to be bribed to come, and no microteaching situation provides genuine *teaching*, but not to peer teach would mean that all discussion would be based on at best videotaped situations which had not been experienced live).

(iii) Those who are 'taught' have the experience of being in the pupil situation and—if they can suspend disbelief—can sense some of the difficulties of that position.

(iv) Some techniques for classroom observation and analysis can be practised without the inconvenience of going to a school.

(v) Most important, we can prepare and discuss teaching in small groups, co-operatively, with a very close relationship between the practice being observed and the discussion and preparation, both in time and the people involved.

This claim does not involve any suggestion of using the technique as a way of 'correcting' or 'improving' specific skills, although it is possible that such results may come as spin-off. The emphasis here is on the microteaching as a source for discussion and analysis, with the general aim of sensitizing students to the process of integrating practical decisions with systematic and principled thinking about both specific teaching demands and general educational theory.

Students microteach from 0930 to 1300 every day. The afternoons and evenings are spent in preparation. As a run-in to the formal microteaching sessions there should have been a great deal of informal small-group practising of specific techniques in the course of normal methods classes. This will have happened twice weekly for the first part of the term—the microteaching takes place towards the end of the first term. The only other formal preparation is a lecture, accompanied by a handout, on some procedures for analysing classroom activity.

The sessions are conducted in order to cover a variety of different procedures, using a framework which gives some cohesion but which allows each group to determine its own needs and strategies to a certain extent. The basic programme is as follows:

Days 1 and 2. All fifteen students teach one individual 'lesson' each of four to five minutes. These are videotaped and played back, either one at a time or in groups of three or four. There is only time for a fairly short discussion after each one, but all students see themselves on videotape.

Days 3 and 4. All fifteen students teach another microlesson. These will probably be videotaped and played back, but the play-back will be selective and students can opt out of being recorded at all. There is much more time for discussion as a result, and reteaching by the original teacher or by others occurs more frequently. Often the choice of topics for Days 3 and 4 arises directly from discussions on the first two days, and groups of students may decide all to approach the same problem from various directions. During these two days fruitful collaboration often develops in the preparation.

Days 5 and 6. Students are divided into five groups of three, and each group has to prepare a twenty-minute extract from a lesson. This may be taught in a variety of ways. One student may teach it, more frequently it will be taught by all three either concurrently or as three separate units, and occasionally one student will teach it but will set up the other two to sit in as pupils with everyone else and to offer specific kinds of support. Discussion from these lessons may be extensive: often more than an hour. It will concentrate on choices made during the lesson. Questions relating to alternative modes of presentation, timing of parts of the lesson and techniques for dealing with particular problems will arise. Where discussion on the first four days will be limited, by the concentration imposed by the time restriction, to matters of technique, discussion of the twenty minute lessons will be much more open ended. Directing this discussion so that it is not too diffuse but not too tutor-centred is extremely difficult.

Day 7. Students will themselves determine the best way of ending the micro-teaching period. Often they will wish to repeat the format of some of the earlier days. I usually insist that at some stage they play an 'improvizing' game, in which each student has to draw a task out of a hat and *immediately* teach as instructed, without time to think. Tasks may be: drill rapidly to sensitize pupils to a /v/-/w/ confusion which has come up, improvize a mime to put life into a class which threatens to collapse into sleep, you have been asked the meaning of 'threatening' —do anything (except define it) to enable the class to understand its meaning. This activity is fun, and helps to reduce tension at the end of a very concentrated period of intensive work.

Types of task. For the short lessons, students are asked to choose from a list of situations originally compiled by Dr Geoffrey Broughton, of which an example is given as follows:

Assignment 11:

> Learners: 14-year-old mixed intermediate.
> Previous knowledge: three years of English.
> Aim: To revise and practise Type 1 conditionals, direct and reported.
> Use: Blackboard story, taped drill, substitution tables, written work.

They are asked to decide whether they are working within the presentation, drilling, controlled practice or free practice part of a unit, and to use a four- or five-minute extract of the lesson. If they feel unhappy with the situations presented (there are 18 in all), they are free to specify their own, using the same format. The tasks for the longer lessons may follow the same basic list, or may be constructed as a result of earlier discussion on the first few days. Sometimes it seems appropriate for a number of students to attempt the same, or related tasks, but no rigid pattern is followed.

Pattern for a particular lesson

There will be four sets of students in any particular lesson: from one to three teaching, from one to three making formal observations at the back of the lesson, probably one working the camera, and the remainder acting as 'pupils'. Normally these roles rotate, at least in the first four days, so that the person who has just taught will operate the camera in the next lesson, become a pupil the next, and possibly observe the next. Students are asked to specify before they teach not only the task, level and type of class and so on, but also what types of observation they would particularly like checked. The lesson is then taught, possibly played back, and the teacher is given first chance to speak. Discussion then follows as much as there is time for, or as is judged necessary, and at an appropriate moment the observers are asked to produce their statistics. In practice, fruitful discussion rarely finishes in less than four times the length of the lesson, and can often go on a great deal longer, especially if demonstration and reteaching is included. Quite often subsequent lessons by the same or other students will directly spring out of the discussion of a particular lesson.

Problems and comments

(a) *The teacher*. Most people are very nervous at first, although a lot depends on the group rapport and supportiveness. It certainly helps for it to be known that everyone has to go through the experience, but all teachers are relieved when the first lesson has been completed. Apart from nervousness, the major problem at first is understanding that a four-minute lesson is a four-minute *extract*, not a forty-minute lesson condensed into four minutes, nor—of course—a four-minute talk about a lesson. Discussion of basic preparation becomes crucial here (but I have avoided showing tapes of microteaching after one disastrous experience when everyone followed the videotapes slavishly after they had been shown).

(b) *The class*. There are various possibilities for class behaviour. I have often found simulation of pupil behaviour very effective, but there is always the risk of the student who is insensitive ruining everything with inappropriate responses. In general, I recommend a fairly deadpan approach, simply serving the ball back, on the first two days, but allow increasing simulation to be introduced gently from then on. It helps here if the teacher sits in with the groups as a pupil, so that the situation does not explode as everyone giggles helplessly—or at least does that less often than it might.

(c) *The camera operator.* Not everyone wants to operate the camera, but most people appreciate the opportunity. The most important techniques to learn is not to move, or zoom, too rapidly. This is pretty soon picked up, but first attempts at camera movement usually result in rather jerky filming.

(d) *The observers.* I usually have one observer for each lesson using the Flanders system, simply because it is much talked about, so that it is useful for people to see how it works. The other one or two either follow the suggestions of the teachers, who want particular features looked at, or their own or my suggestions as we hear what kind of lesson is going to be taught. Sometimes grids are drawn to show direction and number of questions, sometimes careful timing of phases in the lesson, sometimes counts of number of appropriate responses from individual pupils, and so on. Later in the week we may even experiment with less objective procedures, such as grading the lesson on a warm-cold five-point scale. Decisions to use particular observation techniques depend on an understanding of what sort of information the teacher will happily respond to, as well as matters of efficiency. Altogether, the observers contribute usefully to discussion, as well as enabling us to consider the worth of particular procedures. Later, during the full teaching practice in Spain, students will observe each other teach, and they frequently, voluntarily, produce statistics from observation for their own informal discussions.

(e) *The role of the tutor.* I always take part as a pupil, and sometimes teach a lesson. At the beginning I lead the discussion, but later I will take a much less dominant role, occasionally not even contributing at all, perhaps leaving the group altogether for some discussion. The microteaching period is extremely intensive, and can become too tutor-centred, especially when everyone is nervous at the beginning. However, students usually expect me to take a fairly dominant role, and I frequently have more difficulty avoiding responsibility than acquiring it. Particularly, students often want to know whether a particular approach is absolutely satisfactory, and have to be told that nothing is absolutely so—it will always depend on who is teaching whom and where they are. That is, microteaching can help us to do certain things, but it cannot set up patterns which can then be applied uncritically to any outside situation.

There is one problem which is worth mentioning, because I have not been able to solve it. If the tutor has a model of what good teaching is, and imposes it, he breeds confidence, but he is also starting not from a view of where students are, but of where they ought to be. If the tutor says, in effect, 'Show me what you can do, and I will suggest ways of improving it, without stopping you from being you, building on what you have done', then he will appear to be using a deficit model of teaching, because he will be making suggestions for improvement, which imply criticism, without being able to say 'Yes, your good points were close to my model'—because he has not got that sort of model. This difficulty applied mainly to teaching practice, but it arises in microteaching even if the intention is not to improve, because students do want to be praised and commented upon by the end of the period, if not at the beginning. At the moment I attain an uneasy and unsatisfactory compromise between student-centred improvement comment and praise about which I feel guilty. My difficulty is that in microteaching I cannot tell whether anything is good teaching—that will depend on the relationship achieved with the class; I can praise good technique, but such praise is rather limited in value as it is a necessary but not sufficient attainment: I can tell that some things are bad teaching, so I risk appearing negative. This is a problem which I do discuss with students, and indeed I have had no microteaching group which has not had one session voluntarily discussing the whole problem of teacher training.

I hope in this brief description to have shown one way of approaching a microteaching slot in an EFL teacher training programme. My aim has been to be both flexible and principled. Only students can tell whether I ever succeed.

The Decision-making Pyramid and Teacher Training for ELT

(written with Richard Rossner for *English Language Teaching Journal*, **36**, 4, 1982)

The foreign language teaching process, like most human activities, depends on making choices of various kinds: choices of materials, activities, approaches, and so on. Since teaching, like language itself, is necessarily linear, decisions constantly need to be made, sometimes to eliminate alternatives, and sometimes to arrange different activities in a productive order. In this paper, we wish to take an analytical look at this decision-making process and examine the needs behind it, with a view to proposing a hierarchy of decisions. We shall then propose that this hierarchy is not sufficiently respected either in the career structure of the profession itself or during teacher training. Finally, we shall argue for an 'extendible' model of teacher training that takes the decision pyramid into account.

In a classic work on motivation, Maslow proposes that motivational needs should be seen as hierarchically arranged (Maslow, 1970:35ff). According to this 'holistic-dynamic theory of human motivation', primary physiological needs such as hunger must be met (though not necessarily fully satisfied) before second stage 'safety' or security needs are felt; this triggering of higher order motivational needs by the satisfaction of lower order ones continues until the level most significant for education is reached—the need for 'self-actualization' or fulfilment. In other words, the full force of the individual's motivation can only be stimulated by dealing with lower order physiological, psychological and emotional needs which otherwise will act as barriers.

Although such a theory of motivation has implications for language teaching no less than for other sorts of teaching, as Stevick points out (Stevick, 1976: 49ff), we wish in the present paper to focus not so much on learners' motivational needs as on the teacher's methodological needs. Using Maslow's pyramid as a metaphor, it is possible to devise a hierarchy which may be helpful as a means of conceptualizing the development and use of abilities in teaching. Many of these language-teaching needs are included in Strevens's 'model of the language learning and language teaching process' (Strevens, 1977: 35). Under the heading 'teaching' in the central frame of Strevens's model we find: 'approach'; 'pedagogy, methodology, instruction, teaching' (grouped together as the 'element concerned with the presentation to the learner of the material he is learning'); 'syllabus design'; and 'materials construction'. However, no attempt is made in the model to impose any order of importance on these very different elements. Yet clearly their relative status and interrelationship is crucially important if we are, as Strevens suggests, using them to establish a model of the language learning and teaching process.

Let us take the items on Strevens's list and look at each one a little more closely. The first is 'approach', and we find that by this he means: '. . . a commitment to particular, specified points of view, to an ideology . . .' (p.35). This, then, refers to attitudes to relevant linguistic, sociolinguistic, psycholinguistic, pedagogic and other theory. Such attitudes, based on varying degrees of knowledge and experience, will be implicit in any teaching. Some model of language will underly the thinking and explanations or methodological choices of even the most inexpert teacher. Similarly, some model of the nature of learning, of the role of the teacher and of the aims of education will be implicit in any classroom actions.

But, while all teachers inevitably reveal attitudes to such ideological issues, there is no simple manner of selection. We cannot provide a range of options under each heading: democratic/authoritarian, mentalist/behaviourist, serialist/holist, structural/functional, and ask teachers to choose which they prefer. For one thing the relationships between the various choices are complex and the subject of violent debate between theorists; for another, most teachers are unwilling by temperament to engage in such theoretical debate, and many lack either the experience or expertise to make informed choices at this level. In practice, particularly at the beginning of their careers, teachers tend to accept the local tradition as embodied in the practices of teachers already in the field, the existing materials and syllabuses, and the concrete social and political environment.

Now, one of the functions of teacher training, and one of the requirements of a committed and professional teaching profession, we would contend, is a willingness to question and revise fundamental assumptions about the nature of education. But such questioning and revision must be based on a close understanding of the nature of teaching and learning, derived from experience as well as from theory. Making explicit, and consequently making available for questioning, one's own attitudes to ideological issues presupposes that enough experience of teaching has been acquired to enable one's own behaviour to be examined, not merely one's abstract ideas. The modification of these ideas in the light of experience is an essential prerequisite for serious assessment of the value of a particular approach. Consequently, while 'approach' is at a high level of abstraction, it cannot be regarded as the basis for initial decision-making in teaching. We shall return to this point later.

Similar points can be made about Strevens' third and fourth categories. 'Syllabus design' can be placed below 'approach' in the hierarchy. It is a concern of major importance to teachers because within syllabuses the principles embodied in an approach are translated into a sequence of elements suitable for particular groups of students. But without a close acquaintance with students, and considerable experience of their various difficulties and needs, the process of syllabus design will remain abstract, and therefore inappropriate to particular groups of students. 'Materials construction', insofar as it embodies the specific realization of principles of syllabus design, must come next in the hierarchy, and finally the decision-making of a particular teacher in a particular classroom at a particular time. In practice, nearly all the language teachers in the world are concerned primarily with the last to the exclusion of the others, for decisions at the highest three levels are frequently taken outside the classroom.

Let us consider briefly what happens when decisions have to be made. In each case choices will be constrained from above and from below. Decisions made higher up the hierarchy will limit the options lower down, and the conditions under which

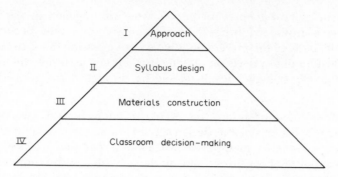

decisions are made lower down will limit freedom to choose higher up. Below the pyramid are the physical, social and emotional actualities of existing classrooms; above and beyond are the principles and aspirations, as well as the abstract generalizations, around which our actions are built. The process of informed decision-making will involve the teacher in investigating what options are open, examining them in the light of decisions made higher up the pyramid and of practical constraints lower down, and choosing the option which will most appropriately mediate between the two. The number and nature of options available to a teacher will depend in part on the amount of practical experience brought to the task, in part on the degree of familiarity with relevant theory, and in part on the sensitivity and talent of the individual.

Two other points should be made about our decision to use a pyramid as a model (rather than, say, a series of stages linked by arrows). One is to do with its shape, which relates both to quantity and influence. The 'higher' decisions not only influence those lower down, but they are made from a more limited range of options. There are only a fairly small number of possible broad approaches to the learning process, while the range of possible materials is enormous, even when practical considerations have been taken into account. Again, decisions are being made all the time at the lower levels (about tone of voice, gesture, changes of technique, and so on), while at the higher levels the process of change is slower and subject to more extended theoretical discussion. The other point is to do with the relationship between the parts. The higher decisions are only made on the foundations of the lower ones. They cannot (or should not) exist without them. This is not to say that basic and local decision-making provides the sole criterion for higher decisions—we have already seen that this is not so. But there is no point in making the higher decisions without the lower foundation. Easing and enabling classroom decision-making to be more effective is the sole justification for decision-making at the higher levels: without the base there can be no apex.

There is, of course, a paradox here, for the pyramid reflects status in the profession. But this is unavoidable. Rarity tends to breed status, and—while we need discussion of possible approaches, alternative syllabuses, and varied materials —we do not need as many people doing these things as we need teachers. The important issue is how to prevent people who are engaged in the higher level decision-making from acquiring their own momentum and becoming merely parasitic on the body of the profession. One way of ensuring this is to be clear about the hierarchical nature of decision-making, for if it is a hierarchy the normal route to decision-making at higher levels should be through decision-making at lower ones.

This brings us to the implications for teacher training. Broadly, we would wish to argue that the practice of syllabus design should not be carried out by those without substantial experience of materials construction, that the practice of materials construction should not be carried out by those without substantial experience of classroom decision-making, and that discussion of approaches to language teaching is best done by those with substantial experience in all the other three spheres. This is not to say that teachers, and student teachers, do not need to understand what happens in the other areas; indeed, we are arguing that an awareness of the relationships between these levels of decision-making is essential. But experience at the lower levels is the most important way of ensuring that what happens at the higher levels neither becomes out of touch with practical possibilities nor becomes exploitative and elite-creating.

The content of teacher training courses, then, would be drawn from all four levels, but the kinds of decision-making expected would vary according to the level and experience of participants. An introductory, pre-service course cannot usefully go beyond helping teachers to start their careers as teaching practitioners. Decision-making must be at Level IV only, though informed decision-making at Level IV will demand an understanding of the processes used by those who make decisions at the other levels. There will of course be decisions to be taken at varying levels of generality within level four: we cannot, for example, make useful decisions about choices of teaching technique until we have decided the objectives for that part of the lesson. But these decisions, while they are hierarchically organized in terms of levels of generality, are not hierarchically organized in relation to needs of teachers, which our pyramid reflects. There is no sense in which we can say that we should not establish aims of lessons until we have mastered individual techniques. Consequently we do not feel that the pyramid can usefully be broken down into more refined categories.

Pre-service courses will vary in length and sophistication, but while they may explore level IV in greater or lesser depth, we do not feel that detailed exploration of levels I-III is appropriate at this stage. Until experience has been gained working with other people's materials, within other people's syllabuses, decisions about what are or are not good materials and syllabuses can only reflect the external views of those who train rather than the internal feelings of students/teachers themselves. Materials construction (which does not of course necessarily require specialized training) is something which should gradually develop out of dissatisfaction *from personal teaching experience* with existing materials, and is inappropriate as a major goal for initial training. (Again, we should emphasize that we are not objecting to the writing of materials during initial courses, in order to enable trainees to understand some of the problems of materials design. We are concerned with the idea that teachers can or should leave initial training courses able and willing to base much of their teaching on materials they write themselves.)

In-service teacher training may be concerned with improving teachers' existing abilities in relation to Level IV, and/or with developing specific practical skills for Levels II and III. Similarly, more academic courses, at Masters level, and of course research, will be concerned with the process of understanding all levels in order to feed in to decision-making at the approach level, Level I—for all theoretical discussion will have major implications for Level I. But there is something strange about encouraging extensive theoretical discussion of a practical activity which has not been extensively experienced by participants. The normal route to Level I should be via Levels IV, III and II.

There is a difference between Level I and the other three lower levels, however, which allows us to welcome outside intervention more than lower down the pyramid. The general ideological issues to which language teaching must ultimately relate cannot be simply technical. It is necessary that discussion of language teaching should be related to wider issues, religious or political or economic or ethical. Just as the base of the pyramid must be securely founded on the actualities of the classroom, so the summit must be exposed to the influence of ideas from external sources; otherwise language teaching may become too inward looking. The normal route to Level I should be via the lower levels, but that should not be the sole route. Unlike lower down the pyramid, we should welcome the views of outsiders at that level, for without the views of outsiders there is a risk of the whole profession becoming self-serving, an elite exploiting the rest of the world, or the rest of the educational profession. But we cannot allow decisions in Level I to be predominantly those of outsiders, for if they are they will lose contact with the necessary expertise which can only be gained through close, routine (and often dull) experience at the lower levels.

This model will allow us to see the teacher training process as a series of layers within the pyramid:

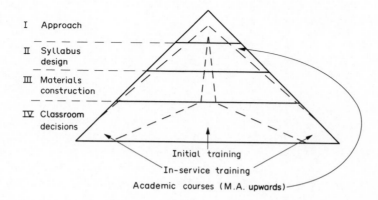

Areas of appropriate concern for teacher training

Only by imposing some coherent, even if slightly artificial, order on the unruly hordes of decisions that pervade language teaching can we give a meaningful direction to our training of language teachers. This model will prevent us training students to run before they can walk, and prevent us seeing language teaching as a body of skills all of equal importance, and all equally accessible to all teachers, no matter what their background or experience.

Bibliography

Abbs, Brian and Malcolm Sexton (1978) *Challenges*, London, Longman.

Abbs, Peter (1969) *English for Diversity*, London, Heinemann.

Alatis, J., H. Altman and P. Alatis (eds.) (1981) *The Second Language Classroom: directions for the 1980s*, New York, Oxford University Press.

Alexander, L. G. *et al*, (1975) *English Grammatical Structure*, London, Longman.

Allen, J. P. B. and S. Pit Corder (eds.) (1973) *The Edinburgh Course in Applied Linguistics*, Vol. 1, Oxford University Press.

Allwright, R. L. (1977) 'Language learning through communication practice', *ELT Documents* 76/3, London, The British Council: 2-14 (reprinted in Brumfit and Johnson, 1979).

Bamgbose, A. (ed.) (1976) *Mother Tongue Education: the West African Experience*, London, Hodder and Stoughton, and Paris, UNESCO.

Barnes, D., J. Britton and H. Rosen (1969) *Language, the Learner and the School*, Harmondsworth, Penguin.

Bernstein, B. (1971) *Class, Codes and Control*, Vol. 1, London, Routledge & Kegan Paul.

Bernstein, B. (1975) *Class, Codes and Control*, Vol. 3, London, Routledge & Kegan Paul.

Blumberg, A. and R. T. Golembiewski (1976) *Learning and Change in Groups*, Harmondsworth, Penguin.

Blunt, Jean (1977) 'Response to reading', *English in Education* **11**, 3.

Bright, J. A. and G. P. McGregor (1970) *Teaching English as a Second Language*, London, Longman.

Brinke, Steven ten (1976) *The Complete Mother Tongue Curriculum*, London, Longman.

Britton, J. (ed.) (1967) *Talking and Writing: a handbook for English teachers*, London, Methuen.

Britton, J. (1970) *Language and Learning*, London, Allen Lane.

Brumfit, Ann (1980) 'The rise and development of a language policy in German East Africa', *Sprache und Geschichte in Afrika* **2**, Hamburg, Helmut Buske Verlag: 219–332.

Brumfit, C. J. (1970) 'Literature teaching in Tanzania', *Journal of the Language Association of Eastern Africa* **1**, 2: 38–44 (reprinted in Brumfit, 1980a).

Brumfit, C. J. (1977), 'Teaching pupils how to acquire language', *ELT Documents* 76/3, London, The British Council: 24–28 (reprinted in Brumfit, 1980a).

Brumfit, C. J. (1978) 'The English language, ideology, and international communication', *ELT Documents* 102, *English as an International Language*, London, The British Council: 15–24 (reprinted in Brumfit, 1980a).

Brumfit, C. J. (1980a) *Problems and Principles in English Teaching*, Oxford, Pergamon Press.

Brumfit, C. J. (1980b) 'Accuracy and fluency', *Practical English Teacher* 1, 3: 6–7 (reprinted in this volume, pp. 9–13).

Brumfit, C. J. (1981a) 'Notional syllabuses revisited: a response', *Applied Linguistics* **2**, 1: 90–92 (reprinted in this volume, pp. 69–72).

Brumfit, C. J. (1981b) 'Teaching the general student', in Johnson and Morrow, 1981: 46–51.

Brumfit, C. J. (1982) 'Some humanistic doubts about humanistic language teaching', *ELT Documents* 113, London, The British Council: 11–19 (reprinted in this volume, pp. 79–85).

Brumfit, C. J. (1984) *Communicative Methodology in Language Teaching*, Cambridge University Press.

Brumfit, C. J. and Keith Johnson (eds.) (1979) *The Communicative Approach to Language Teaching*, Oxford University Press.

Bullock, Alan (1975) *A Language for Life*: Report of the committee of inquiry to the Secretary of State for Education and Science, London, HMSO.

Canale, Michael and Merrill Swain (1980) 'Theoretical bases of communicative approaches to second language teaching and testing', *Applied Linguistics*, **1**, 1: 1–47.

Canham, W. (ed.) (1972) *Mother-tongue Teaching*, Hamburg Institute for Education, UNESCO.

Carroll, Lewis (1872) *Through the Looking Glass*, London, Macmillan.

Carver, D. and M. Wallace (1977) 'Models of microteaching in the training of language teachers', mimeo, Scottish Centre for Education Overseas, Moray House, Edinburgh.

Cole, P. and J. Morgan (eds.) (1975) *Syntax and Semantics*, Vol. 3, *Speech Acts*, New York, Academic Press.

Corder, S. Pit (1973) *Introducing Applied Linguistics*, Harmondsworth, Penguin.

Corder, S. Pit (1978) 'Learner language and teacher talk', *Audio-Visual Language Journal* **16**, 1: 5–13.

Corder, S. Pit (1981) *Error Analysis and Interlanguage*, Oxford University Press.

Coste, Daniel *et al* (1976) *Un Niveau-Seuil*, Strasbourg, Council of Europe.

Culler, Jonathon (1975) *Structuralist Poetics*, London, Routledge & Kegan Paul.

Curran, C. (1976) *Counselling-learning in Second Language Learning*, New York, Apple River Press.

Derrick, June (1966) *Teaching English to Immigrants*, London, Longman.

Dixon, John (1967) *Growth through English* (2nd edition 1975), Oxford University Press.

Feyerabend, Paul (1975) *Against Method*, London, Verso.

Flower, F. D. (1966) *Language in Education*, London, Longman.

Freire, Paulo (1971) *Pedagogy of the Oppressed*, trans. from Portugese by Myra Bergman Ramos, New York, Herder and Herder (original Portugese, 1968).

Gattegno, Caleb (1972) *Teaching Foreign Languages in Schools: The Silent Way* (2nd edition), New York, Educational Solutions Inc. (1st ed., 1963).

Gattegno, Caleb (1976) *Common Sense of Foreign Language Teaching*, New York, Educational Solutions Inc.

Giles, H. (ed.) (1977) *Language, Ethnicity and Intergroup Relations*, London, Academic Press.

Gore, M. Lesley (1978) 'Review of extensive readers', *ARELS Journal* **2**, 10, 255.

Grice, H. (1975) 'Logic and conversation', in Cole and Morgan, 1975: 41–58.

Gubbay, Denise and Sheila Coghill (1980) *Speak for Yourself: making language work for you*, London, BBC.

Halliday, M. A. K. (1967) 'Linguistics and the teaching of English', in Britton, 1967: 80–90.

Halliday, M. A. K. (1973) *Explorations in the Functions of Language*, London, Edward Arnold.

Halliday, M. A. K. (1975) *Learning How to Mean*, London, Edward Arnold.

Halliday, M. A. K. (1976) '"The teacher taught the student English": an essay in applied linguistics', The Second LACUS Forum, Columbia, S.Carolina, Hornbeam Press: 344–349.

Halliday, M. A. K. (1979) 'Development of texture in child language', in Myers, 1979.

Harris, Roy (1980) *The Language-Makers*, Ithaca, New York, Cornell University Press.

Hinde, R. (1972) *Non-verbal Communication*, Cambridge University Press.

Hinde, R. (1979) *Towards Understanding Relationships*, London, Academic Press.

Hindmarsh, Roland (1980) *Cambridge English Lexicon*, Cambridge University Press.

Holbrook, David (1961) *English for Maturity*, Cambridge University Press.

Holbrook, David (1964) *English for the Rejected*, Cambridge University Press.

Hollindale, P. (1972) 'Why have things gone wrong?' (book review), *The Use of English* **23**, 4: 334–336.

James, C. V. (ed.) (1978) *The Older Mother Tongues of the United Kingdom*, London, Centre for Information on Language Teaching and Research.

Johnson, Keith (1982), *Communicative Syllabus Design and Methodology*, Oxford, Pergamon Press.

Johnson, Keith and Keith Morrow (eds.) (1978) *Functional Materials and the Classroom Teacher*, Reading, Centre for Applied Language Studies.

Johnson, Keith and Keith Morrow (eds.) (1981) *Communication in the Classroom*, London, Longman.

Jupp, T. C. *et al* (1979), *Encounters*, London, Heinemann.

Jupp, T. C. and S. Hodlin (1975) *Industrial English*, London, Heinemann.

Kennedy, B. H. (1930) *Revised Latin Primer*, London, Longman.

Kovel, J. (1976) *A Complete Guide to Therapy*, Harmondsworth, Penguin.

Krashen, Stephen D. (1976) 'Formal and informal linguistic environments in language learning and language acquisition', *TESOL Quarterly* **10**, 2: 157–168.

Krashen, Stephen D. (1981), *Second Language Acquisition and Second Language Learning*, Oxford, Pergamon Press.

Kucera, H. and W. Nelson Francis (1967) *Computational Analysis of Present-day American English*, Rhode Island, Brown University Press.

Labov, W. (1972) *Sociolinguistic Patterns*, Philadelphia, University of Pennsylvania Press.

Leavis, F. R. (1933) *For Continuity*, Cambridge, Minority Press.

Leavis, F. R. and Denys Thompson (1933) *Culture and Environment*, London, Chatto & Windus.

Leontiev, Alexei A. (1981) *Psychology and the Language Learning Process* (translated by J. Curtis from Russian), Oxford, Pergamon Press.

Linden, E. (1975) *Apes, Men and Language*, Harmondsworth, Penguin.

Lozanov, Georgi (1978) *Suggestology and Outlines of Suggestopedy*, trans. from Bulgarian by Marjorie Hall-Pozharlieva and Krassimira Pashmakova, London, Gordon & Breach (original ed. 1971, Nauki i Izkustvi, Sofia).

Lyons, John (1972) 'Human language', in Hinde, 1972: 49–85.

Mackay, Ronald, Bruce Barkman and R. R. Jordan (eds.) (1979) *Reading in a Second Language*, Rowley Mass., Newbury House.

Mackey, W. F. (1965) *Language Teaching Analysis*, London, Longman.

Maley, Alan and Alan Duff (1978) *Drama Techniques in Language Learning*, Cambridge University Press.

Marshall, Julia (1972) *European Curriculum Studies* 5: *The Mother Tongue*, Strasbourg, Council of Europe.

Maslow, A. (1970) *Motivation and Personality*, New York, Harper & Row.

Melville, Maggie *et al.* (1980) *Towards the Creative Teaching of English*, London, George Allen & Unwin.

Mill, John Stuart (1873) *Autobiography* (cited from Columbia University Press edition of 1924).

Mitchell, Rosamond, Brian Parkinson and Richard Johnstone (1981). *The Foreign Language Classroom: an observational study*, Stirling Educational Monographs No. 9, Department of Education, University of Stirling.

Moskowitz, Gertrude (1978), *Caring and Sharing in the Foreign Language Class*, Rowley Mass., Newbury House.

Muller, Kurt E. (ed.) (1980) *The Foreign Language Syllabus and Communicative Approaches to Teaching*, special issue of *Studies in Second Language Acquisition* **3**, 1.

Munby, John (1968) *Read and Think*, London, Longman (introduction reprinted in Mackay, Barkman and Jordan, 1979).

Munby, John (1978) *Communicative Syllabus Design*, Cambridge University Press.

Myers, T. (ed.) (1979) *The Development of Conversation and Discourse*, Edinburgh University Press.

Naiman, N. *et al.* (1978) *The Good Language Learner*, Research in Education Series No. 7, Toronto, Ontario Institute for Studies in Education.

Newmark, L. (1966) 'How not to interfere with language learning', *International Journal of American Linguistics* **32**, 1, II: 77–83 (reprinted in Brumfit and Johnson, 1979).

O'Connell, Peter (1982) 'Suggestopedy and the adult language learner', *ELT Documents* 113, London, The British Council: 110–117.

Pettit, R. D. (1971) 'Literature in East Africa', *Journal of the Language Association of Eastern Africa* **2**, 1.

Pickett, G. D. (1978) *The Foreign Language Learning Process*, London, The British Council.

Popper, Karl (1957) *The Poverty of Historicism*, London, Routledge & Kegan Paul.

Popper, Karl (1972) *Objective Knowledge*, Oxford University Press.

Popper, Karl (1976) *Unended Quest*, London, Collins, Fontana.

Richterich, R. and J. L. Chancerel (1977) *Identifying the Needs of Adults Learning a Foreign Language*, Strasbourg, Council of Europe.

Rivers, Wilga M. (1972) *Speaking with Many Tongues*, Rowley Mass., Newbury House.

Roberts, P. (1964) *English Syntax*, New York, Harcourt Brace & World.

Rogers, Carl (1969) *Freedom to Learn*, Columbia Ohio, Charles E. Merrill.

Rogers, Sinclair (ed.) (1976) *They Don't Speak Our Language*, London, Edward Arnold.

Rosen, Harold (1978) 'Signing on', *The New Review*, February, reprinted in *BAAL Newsletter* **7**, June 1979.

Rosen, Harold and Tony Burgess (1980) *Languages and Dialects of London Schoolchildren*, London, Ward Lock.

Schumann, John H. (1978) *The Pidginization Process*, Rowley Mass., Newbury House.

Scovell, Thomas (1979) Review of Lozanov, 'Suggestology and outlines of suggestopedy', *TESOL Quarterly* **13**, 2: 255–266.

Searle, Chris (1972) *The Forsaken Lover*, London, Routledge & Kegan Paul.

Shaw, A. M. (1977) 'Foreign-language syllabus development: some recent approaches', *Language Teaching and Linguistics Abstracts* **10**, 4: 217–233.

Simon, Sidney B., L. Howe and Howard Kirschenbaum (1972) *Values Clarification: a practical handbook of strategies for teachers and students*, New York, Hart.

Spolsky, B. (1978) *Educational Linguistics*, Rowley Mass., Newbury House.

Stevick, Earl W. (1976) *Memory, Meaning and Method*, Rowley Mass., Newbury House.

Stevick, Earl W. (1980) *Teaching Languages: a Way and Ways*, Rowley Mass., Newbury House.

Stevick, Earl W. (1982) *Teaching and Learning Languages*, Cambridge University Press.

Stratta, L., J. Dixon and A. Wilkinson (1973), *Patterns of Language*, London, Heinemann.

Strevens, Peter (1977) *New Orientations in the Teaching of English*, Oxford University Press.

Stubbs, Michael (1976) *Language, Schools and Classrooms*, London, Methuen.

Thomson, Jack (1979) 'Response to reading: the process as described by one fourteen-year-old', *English in Education* **13**, 3.

Thorndike, E. L. and I. Lorge (1944) *The Teacher's Wordbook of 30,000 Words*, New York, Teacher's College Columbia.

Trudgill, P. (1975) *Accent, Dialect and School*, London, Edward Arnold.

Ur, Penny (1981) *Discussion that Work*, Cambridge University Press.

van Ek, J. A. (1975) *The Threshold Level*, Strasbourg, Council of Europe (reprinted by Pergamon, Oxford, 1980).

Watson, J. D. (1968) *The Double Helix*, London, Weidenfeld & Nicolson.

West, Michael (1953) *A General Service List of English Words*, London, Longman.

West, Michael (1964) 'Criteria in the selection of simplified reading books', *English Language Teaching* **18**, 4: 146–151.

Whitehead, Frank *et al.* (1977) *Children and their Books*, London, Macmillan.

Widdowson, H. G. (with J. Dakin and B. Tiffen) (1968) *Language in Education*, Oxford University Press.

Widdowson, H. G. (1978) *Teaching Language as Communication*, Oxford University Press.

Widdowson, H. G. (1979) *Explorations in Applied Linguistics*, Oxford University Press.

Widdowson, H. G. and C. J. Brumfit (1981) 'Issues in second language syllabus design', in Alatis, Altman and Alatis, 1981: 197–210.

Wilkins, D. A. (1972a) *Linguistics in Language Teaching*, London, Edward Arnold.

Wilkins, D. A. (1972b) 'Grammatical, situational and notional syllabuses', in *Proceedings of the Third International Congress of Applied Linguistics*, Copenhagen 1972, Julius Groos Verlag, Heidelberg (cited from reprint in Brumfit and Johnson, 1979).

Wilkins, D. A. (1974) 'Notional syllabuses and the concept of a minimum adequate grammar', in *Linguistic Insights in Applied Linguistics*, ed. S. P. Corder and E. Roulet, AIMAV/Didier (cited from reprint in Brumfit and Johnson, 1979).

Wilkins, D. A. (1976) *Notional Syllabuses*, Oxford University Press.

Wilkins, D. A. (1981) 'Notional syllabuses revisited', *Applied Linguistics* **2**, 1: 83–89.

Wilkinson, Andrew (1971) *Foundations of Language*, Oxford University Press.

Wilkinson, Andrew (1975) *Language and Education*, Oxford University Press.

Winch, Peter (1958) *The Idea of a Social Science*, London, Routledge & Kegan Paul.

Wright, C. W. (1965) *An English Word Count*, Pretoria, National Bureau of Education and Social Research.

Index